D0325530

Contents

Contents

A
FIRM
FOUNDATION

A
FIRM
FOUNDATION

*hope and vision for
a new methodist future*

 Seedbed

Printed in the United States of America

Cover design by Nick Perreault at Strange Last Name
Page design by PerfecType, Nashville, Tennessee

A firm foundation : hope and vision for a new Methodist future - Frankin, Tennessee : Seedbed Publishing, ©2017.

pages ; cm. + 1 videodisc

Foreword / William J. Abraham - 1. Commitment to transformation / Jeff Greenway - Witness. Awakening orthodoxy / Madeline Carrasco Henners -2. When Jesus is Lord / David Watson - Witness. Living and relevant church today / Carlos Pirona - 3. Faithfully engaging the scriptures / Chris Ritter - Witness. Committed to scripture / Debo Onabanjo — 4. When the Holy Spirit comes with fire / Carolyn Moore - Witness. Hiring a sanctified felon / Heather Hill - 5. Loving God with an undivided heart / Maxie Dunnam - Witness. Our God of deliverance / Kenneth Levingston - 6. The dynamism of discipleship / Andrew Forrest - Witness. Jesus on the margins / Jorge Acevedo - 7. The church's global DNA / Kimberly Reisman - Witness. Agenda at the crossroads / Jerry Kulah - Epilogue. What comes next? / Keith Boyette.

Includes bibliographical references.
ISBN 9781628245110 (paperback : alk. paper)
ISBN 9781628245158 (DVD)
ISBN 9781628245127 (Mobi)
ISBN 9781628245134 (ePub)
ISBN 9781628245141 (uPDF)

1. Methodist Church—Doctrines. 2. Church renewal—Methodist Church.

BX8331.3.F57 2017   230/.7   2017954718

 Seedbed

SEEDBED PUBLISHING
Franklin, Tennessee
seedbed.com

Foreword

I had never wanted to go to Jerusalem or to the Holy Land. A lot of folk have been puzzled when they discovered that this was the case. My reasoning was simple: the risen Lord is present everywhere so there is no need to travel to the Holy Land; we occupy holy spaces here where we are and where we seek the Spirit's grace. Then I was invited to attend a conference in Jerusalem led by Jewish philosophers, and I decided to go. After ten days there, I cannot wait to get back. Three things caught my attention; some of the holy sites, especially the Garden Tomb and the Sea of Galilee; the amazing intellectualism and spiritual fecundity of the Jewish scholars I met; and the remarkable achievements (warts and all) of the state of Israel over the last seventy years. I am glad that I got over my hesitations.

Many of us have similar hesitations about the journey ahead of us in United Methodism. We would prefer to stay where we are, minister to the people the Lord has called us to serve, and finish our work in peace. However, the next Methodism is already around the corner; we cannot sit on the sidelines. More dramatically, the crowbar of events within our church has awakened us from our complacency and slumber, and we must move forward in faith and hope to a new future.

This splendid set of essays is a great place to begin. They represent a sea change in our orientation. Every one of them is written with grace and hope; the days of hand-wringing and lament are over. Every one of them speaks to an issue we need to ponder; there is no shirking the new challenges to be met. Every one of them is written with grace and wit; there is not a hint of polemic or agitation. Every one of them is clear and to the point; there is no doublespeak or sail-trimming.

We have started a long-haul conversation that will continue for years to come. Within this, there are and will be disagreements. But the table is set. All are welcome to work through to a new phase of our history. We need a combination of firmness and flexibility; of impatience and patience; of fear and confidence; and of divine wisdom and human ingenuity. Above all, we need to get our act together in mission and evangelism. There is no need to rush to immediate decisions on the organizational horizon; we will be given the grace needed to cross whatever bridge lies ahead. The road ahead will at times be extremely difficult and even treacherous; the destination, however, will open up a new day for a fresh expression of classical Methodism and of the Evangelical United Brethren tradition.

John Wesley once noted that, whatever happened in the future, God would not allow what he had achieved through Methodism to vanish from the face of the earth. This was not pious sentimentality in operation. It was a serious theological assertion grounded in the fact that Methodism, like the church down through the ages, is created and sustained by the work of the Holy Spirit. Where the Spirit is, there is the church. To be sure, folk will disagree on how to work this out in practice, but this is no excuse for diffidence or despair. We have to take our stand and get on with the light God has given us.

This is not easy when critics misrepresent our convictions and motives. Wesley was no stranger to this; right up until the end he was called all sorts of names and accused of all sorts of errors. To be sure, he made some errors; and we shall too. However, we know that we have come to a crossroads in United Methodism, and we have rightly taken our stand on the moral faith of the Scriptures and of the church through the ages. It is time to move on and work for a fully faithful commitment to Christ and to find fresh expressions for the tradition we inhabit.

We leave to Providence those who disagree with us.

The progressive wing of United Methodism will no doubt flourish in various parts of the United States. Its adherents will render sterling service in some areas of the church's comprehensive mission. They will find a niche in the complex religious landscape of the nation, even as they risk becoming the chaplain to the Left in American politics. However, they will not be able to hold the line morally or theologically and will continue to fly with, if not provide sourcing, for the progressive winds of the culture with enthusiasm.

The so-called centrists will also find preliminary traction because they offer an initially tempting display of tolerance and diversity. They will appeal to the fairmindedness of United Methodists and readily paint their critics as extremists. However, they will have enormous difficulty getting beyond their rhetoric. They have no center of gravity of their own; their position is entirely relative to the contrasting positions at hand. Given the current drive beyond diversity to intersectionality (the jargon for whatever new multiple of identity groups that emerge), they will soon find themselves between a rock and a hard place. Moreover, once it becomes known that most of their leaders are closet progressives, they will have to face the full effects of their confusion and obfuscation.

What we need is a whole new configuration of United Methodism that will be missionary oriented, open to the full working of the Holy Spirit, unapologetically orthodox, sacramentally robust, and committed to justice and the care of the needy. In the short term, we may be a minority in the United States; worldwide, we are likely to be a global majority. I have every confidence in the new generation of leaders who are emerging; some of them are represented in this volume. However, this is not a matter of numbers; it is a simple matter of commitment to truth and grace.

There is also a wider context to consider. My own work and ministry have been devoted to tackling the deep opposition to Christianity that has emerged both in Europe and North America over the last two centuries. Some of this work is high-octane academic work; some of it is teaching and preaching in my local church and in select missionary work abroad. In my own field of research, we face formidable challenges from renewed efforts to undermine the great faith of the church. Over against this, the tide has turned in some circles (most surprisingly in philosophy); it is the opposition that has grown ignorant and paranoiac. It is time for United Methodists to recover their nerve, for its members and scholars to dig deep into the resources God has given us in our heritage, and for all of us to lean into the new resources that the Holy Spirit will supply. It is also time for us to stand with other brothers and sisters in the wider culture in articulation and defense of the faith, not least in its moral commitments.

There is a new Jerusalem and new promised land up ahead of us. I will not live to see the full contours of its landscape. However, these essays give us a constructive glimpse of what is coming in the next Methodism. I am delighted to commend these to your attention. In the meantime, I still hope to see the streets of the old Jerusalem again in the near future!

–William J. Abraham
Outler Professor of Wesley Studies and University
Distinguished Teaching Professor
Perkins School of Theology, Southern Methodist University

Commitment to Transformation

Jeff Greenway

Preach the word; be prepared in season and out of season; correct, rebuke and encourage—with great patience and careful instruction. For the time will come when people will not put up with sound doctrine. Instead, to suit their own desires, they will gather around them a great number of teachers to say what their itching ears want to hear. They will turn their ears away from the truth and turn aside to myths. But you, keep your head in all situations, endure hardship, do the work of an evangelist, discharge all the duties of your ministry.

—2 Timothy 4:2-5

I am not afraid that the people called Methodists should ever cease to exist either in Europe or America. But I am afraid, lest they should only exist as a dead sect, having the form of religion without the power. And this undoubtedly will be the case, unless they hold fast both the doctrine, spirit, and discipline with which they first set out.

—John Wesley in "Thoughts on Methodism" (August 4, 1786)

Everyone has participated in difficult, but necessary conversations about touchy subjects in their lives. It is hard to talk about some things in a marriage, on the job, or in a friendship, but we know that talking about them in the context of love and trust can make them opportunities to strengthen our relationships. As a lifelong pastor, I can testify that some of these difficult discussions can lead to the healthiest of relationships. I can also confirm that they are rarely easy.

As the pastor of a growing and vibrant United Methodist congregation, I want to talk to you about the present state and future direction of our denomination. Currently, our church is in a time of open schism and crisis. Some observers believe that we are living in an era similar to the one Paul wrote about in 2 Timothy 4, where some in the church have "not put up with sound doctrine," and have been turned "away from the truth and turn aside to myths." There are also signs that we may have become what John Wesley feared the Methodist movement would become: "a dead sect, having the form of religion without the power."

In the midst of this somber diagnosis, we also believe in resurrection and that the same power that raised Jesus from the dead lives in us (see Romans 8:11). Resurrecting power can renew and transform our denomination if we will repent and refocus our lives on Jesus.

We believe in resurrection power because we see its evidence in the global movement of vibrant and vital Wesleyan Christianity. One need only look at the growth of Methodism in Africa, South Korea, Cuba, South America, Vietnam, and the Philippines to note that our doctrine, practices, and message can have an incredible impact in the lives of individuals and entire people groups when it is lived in its unfettered and most robust form. In those regions, the Wesleyan movement is flourishing.

Sadly, that is not the case everywhere. The United Methodist Church has dramatically lost membership in the United States for the last fifty years. The reasons for this can be read about elsewhere, but the reality is that many in our connection have wandered far from what Wesley called for when the Methodist movement was spreading scriptural holiness across the land.

Recent events in the life of our denomination have accentuated the growing divide in faith and practice in our church. In our most recent history, we engaged in a process of discernment and decision-making that we agreed to abide by as a denomination. Today, there are segments of our church—clergy, laity, congregations, Annual and Jurisdictional Conferences, and even bishops—who are openly practicing an expression of Christian faith that is defiantly contrary to our agreed-upon covenant and polity. These actions have exposed massive cracks in the foundation of our theology and ministry.

Many pastors and local churches have avoided discussing what is happening in the denomination because their congregations reflect our culture and want to avoid conflict. Others have shied away from discussing it in the noble effort to protect their people from the pain of this larger conversation.

Many evangelical, orthodox United Methodists have spent their lives sharing the saving faith of Jesus, making disciples, reaching out to the outcast and marginalized, and growing their congregations. They have been loyal to their ordination vows, kept their covenantal promises, and paid their apportionments. They pastor warm-hearted and Jesus-loving congregations. They have celebrated the great things United Methodists have done together, such as providing disaster response through the United Methodist Committee on Relief (UMCOR), the building of Africa University, and establishing Imagine No Malaria. However, they have also shielded their congregations from the theological drift away from historic, orthodox, Wesleyan Christianity and the recent acceleration of acts of ecclesial disobedience.

I was once in the same place. While I have been involved in serving in our denomination beyond my local church in my Annual Conference and at the general church level, the main focus of my ministry has been in the congregations and places I have led. There was a time I was not convinced our denominational discord would affect me and my people. I thought that the polity of the church would be honored and held. I did not have the conversation about the developing schism within the denomination in my local church. However, I was wrong.

With increasing regularity, our denomination has begun to show the manifestations of being torn away from what has held us together—our common, agreed-upon covenant. When the denominational news started making the front page of our local newspaper, and was talked about on the nightly news of our local television stations because of celebrated acts of ecclesial disobedience, I was forced to begin to find language and ways to have a discussion with my congregation. We started privately at first with our elected and influential leadership. We then began to have congregational conversation forums where information could be shared, questions asked, and grace shown. Few of our congregations are monolithic; we have a wide variety of opinions in our pews. There is, however, a way to provide helpful leadership in the face of this denominational crisis. Conversations can be held and congregations can move forward together.

The Symptom

Some would say that the cause of the schism is our growing differences on human sexuality. While this topic grabs the headlines, human sexuality is merely the presenting symptom of much deeper theological fissures and systemic problems that are dividing the United Methodist Church.

There are those who no longer support the orthodox belief that Jesus is the way, the truth, and the life—the only way to the Father. In other words, there are those who no longer believe Jesus is who he said he is. There are those who undermine the nature, diminish the role, and gut the authority of Scripture in favor of their own personal experience. There are those who no longer hold to our theology of personal sin, and neglect what salvation means in the

Wesleyan tradition. There are those who have a misappropriated allegiance to the institutional church and have forgotten that our church only has power and standing as we are faithful to the mission and message of Jesus Christ. We have also developed a denominational system with no means of holding those who lead or serve in it accountable. We are fast becoming a church with "the form of religion, without the power" that results in life transformation.

Commitment to Transformation

In order to face a faithful future, our churches must be willing to offer new life in Christ and walk men and women through the not-always-easy steps of transformation. Let me give you an example. Carly and Jim had a past when they began coming to our congregation. While outward appearances might have seemed to be the epitome of success, their marriage was in trouble. Over time, a wall of anger and bitterness had built between them. They came to our congregation because they saw some positive things happening in the lives of some of their friends, and they wanted what they had.

They began to attend worship and Bible study weekly, and those around them could see the wall they had started building around each other begin to crumble. However, it was not until they went on the Walk to Emmaus that God began to do the deepest healing work in their lives. Carly confided that she had been sexually abused as a young girl, which had fractured her self-esteem. She also confessed that she had an abortion when she and Jim were dating. The wall of bitterness that was being built brick by brick on her side was because of her increasing anger toward Jim for wanting her to get an abortion and the lack of worth she felt because her identity had been violated. When she placed those at the feet of Jesus, it opened a pathway to healing that now has her sharing her story and guiding other post-abortive women on the journey of healing and wholeness.

The bitterness between them had manifested itself in alcohol and pornography addiction in Jim. He used the distance from Carly to justify his behavior, but the result was the building of the wall between them on his side. When he was able to lay his addictive behaviors at the feet of Jesus, the deeper path of healing and wholeness began for him. He is now living a life in recovery, and is a leader in our men's ministry.

There is nothing about Carly and Jim's story that came easy. Along the way, the local church was there to hold them in their brokenness and rejoice in their newfound freedom. Ultimately, the local church—through the power of the Holy Spirit—was there to help them walk into their transformed future together. This is our Wesleyan legacy and, more important, this the benchmark of the ministry of Jesus.

The Stretch and Pull

While many in our denomination hold fast to our historically evangelical foundations, others have continually shifted further and further away from our original moorings. One way to envision the current struggle within the United Methodist Church is that of a stretched rubber band. Although we have always had tugging back and forth between conservatives and liberals within the denomination, the leadership of the church has decidedly shifted to the Left—away from transformational Wesleyan Christianity—and pulled the church in that direction. The leftward direction may have appeared to be incremental, but the pull of their influence is unmistakable. The result has been a pulling of the center of the church to the Left.

Thankfully, there have been evangelical brothers and sisters that faithfully drove a stake in the ground around the essentials of biblical, orthodox Wesleyan Christianity, which has anchored one end of that rubber band for the last fifty years. As forces within and outside the United Methodist Church have continued to pull the denomination to the Left, the traditionalist anchor has held firm. Unfortunately, the result of that pull is that the covenant of the church is being stretched to its breaking point.

In recent years, there has been a grassroots pulling back toward a traditional biblical Wesleyan anchor in our activities at General Conference. That is not to say that all things have gone our way, but there are more traditional United Methodists wanting to make their voices heard. As the United Methodist Church has appeared more orthodox in its belief, practice, and polity, progressives that have controlled the larger systems and structures have seen their power base diminish as the denomination changes. The result has been a season of unprecedented disobedience and breaking of our common covenant by individuals, congregations, Annual and Jurisdictional Conferences, and bishops. As the progressive Left has run through the stop signs of the covenant, those with a more traditional view have rallied to the stake placed in the ground around historic Wesleyan orthodoxy.

There has been a renewed rally for those who share a similar view of the life, death, and resurrection of Jesus, and the nature and role of Scripture as has been embraced by the mainstream of Christianity for two thousand years. These brothers and sisters embrace a Wesleyan understanding of sin, and the need for salvation that begins to be reflected in holiness of heart and life. They believe in ministry outside the church walls with the poor and downtrodden, embracing a thoughtful faith that warms and changes the heart and works itself out in social justice that is connected to personal holiness.

On the other end of this stressed and stretched rubber band of the United Methodism spectrum is another group with whom we share increasingly little in common. The result is a deeply divided church where we often use the same words, cite the same Scriptures, quote the same Wesley sermons, and pledge fidelity to the same *Book of Discipline*, but we are talking about *very different* expressions of Christian faith. We are miles apart in basic beliefs and practices—with no real means of accountability—making our covenantal relationship untenable.

Once again, let me be clear, human sexuality is not the cause of our differences. It is merely the presenting symptom. The real cause of our division is related to what we believe about Jesus; the nature, role, and authority of Scripture; the nature of personal sin and salvation; and the work of sanctification in the life and conduct of a follower of Jesus. This is not just about orthodoxy or "right beliefs"—it is also about orthopraxy or "right actions." In response, we need to have both a theological renewal and a movement of the Holy Spirit in the living of our faith.

As United Methodists, we either have to find a way to step back from our irreconcilable visions, or we need to find a way we can separate for the sake of the mission.

The Opportunity

While I pray that our denomination will find a way to right itself and restore the order of our covenant, we very well may be at a Paul-and-Barnabas moment as a denomination. Although the circumstances are uniquely different from our current divisions, we might find wisdom in the way Paul and Barnabas ultimately resolved their dispute. In Acts, Paul's partner on his first missionary journey was Barnabas, the "son of encouragement." He was the first person to embrace and support Paul when he returned to Jerusalem after his Damascus Road conversion. John Mark was a young companion on that first trip. However, John Mark went home early.

Later, in Acts 15, Paul and Barnabas secured the blessing of the Jerusalem Council to take the gospel to the Gentiles and prepared to leave on their second missionary journey from Antioch. It was a pivotal moment in the Christian movement. Paul and Barnabas had a sharp disagreement over John Mark. Barnabas wanted to give his cousin, John Mark, a second chance and take him along. Paul did not. This disagreement had the potential to derail the mission, stopping it dead in its tracks.

However, Paul and Barnabas didn't allow their personal disagreement to derail the mission. Paul took Silas and went off to missionary fame. Barnabas took John Mark, and we never heard about Barnabas again. However, he did what he did best by pouring his life into helping John Mark answer his call.

One of the most remarkable things about that story is what happened to John Mark. He became the traveling companion with Simon Peter, and eventually wrote the Gospel of Mark. Later, Paul would write Timothy and tell him to bring Mark with him because he was helpful to him (see 2 Timothy 4:11). Paul also writes about Mark (the cousin of Barnabas) being with him while he is under house arrest awaiting trial in Rome (see Colossians 4:10).

For the sake of the mission, they went their separate ways. I contend we are at a Paul-and-Barnabas moment. We shouldn't allow our inner squabbling to jeopardize the mission. It may be better served if we bless each other, separate, and see what God does when pursuing the mission once again becomes central.

It is unknown what the "next" for the United Methodist Church will exactly look like, but be assured that the denomination that has nurtured us to this point will look very different in the very near future. If that kind of change is coming, those who share the same heart for a renewed and vibrant expression of evangelical, orthodox Wesleyan Christianity should join together in planning what we need to do to reform our church in order to see transformation in our personal lives and local congregations.

Steps to Reformation

Let me suggest four actions that could help reform our church, and give us confidence for the future.

Refocus on Jesus

As the Bible makes clear, there is no other name by which people can be saved. I have a friend who continually reminds me to focus on Jesus. At first, it was annoying, but then I began to think differently. I began to notice how little Jesus was mentioned at denominational gatherings—except at the end of a prayer. I began to notice how my own preaching became much more effective when I lifted up the name of Jesus. I experienced how bewildering ministry can become when we take our focus off of Jesus. Ministry can be a grind, but too frequently we rely upon what we can do in our own strength, and we forget about the power that is available in Jesus.

The Bible declares that there is no power in any other name than Jesus. Institutions do not save the world; Jesus does. Right theology will not reform the church or save the world; Jesus does. Similarly, winning the right votes at General Conference will not reform the church or save the world; Jesus does.

We need to reclaim the sure and certain belief that Jesus is who he said he is and did everything he said he would do. Jesus lives. Jesus loves. Jesus names sin. Jesus announces grace. Jesus redeems. Jesus saves. Jesus forgives. Jesus heals. Jesus transforms. Jesus sanctifies. Jesus calls. The future will be determined by whether we refocus on Jesus as the way, the truth, and the life.

Reclaim the Authority of Scripture

Either the Bible is the sufficient rule of faith and practice, or it is not. Dr. Albert Outler was one of the greatest thinkers and theologians in the history of the Wesleyan movement. When he developed the Wesleyan Quadrilateral, it was meant to be a framework to help Methodists learn how to work out their salvation and live faith in our world. It has helped to shape our theologizing for fifty years. However, toward the end of his life, he regretted what it had become.

Outler said that there were four sides to this theological decision-making framework: Scripture, tradition, reason, and experience. The challenge comes with where one places Scripture in the Quadrilateral. To Wesley, Scripture was always primary. When the Bible speaks clearly about a subject, tradition, reason, and experience should all be subject to Scripture. This is the view held by most evangelical United Methodists.

While we bring who we are to the reading of the text, orthodox Methodists attempt to understand the text within the original context. When I read something in Scripture that is contrary to an action or attitude within my life experience, that is called sin and through the power of the Holy Spirit, I can receive forgiveness and bring that area of my life under the leadership of Jesus.

Unfortunately, Outler's model is misused by some United Methodists. For them, Scripture is one of four opinions to consider, but is not necessarily primary in the decision-making process. Some actually believe that God is still giving revelation today with the same authority as the canon of the Scriptures. This ultimately replaces or supersedes the Bible. In other words, if an attitude or action in their lived experience contradicts what the Bible clearly teaches, then they feel free to reimagine the Scriptures to fit their present context. Not surprisingly, there is a very different interpretation and application of Scripture when one takes the liberty of reading one's experience into the text.

Refine Our Theology

Yesteryear's theological pluralism of "big tent" Methodism watered down and gutted our robust heritage of evangelical theology and practice of our Wesleyan movement. Because of it, our denomination no longer has a clear theological core and identity. Within limits, theological diversity can be a good thing and stretch us beyond ourselves. After all, orthodox Christianity welcomes and embraces high-church folks, charismatics, and contemporary-worship-style evangelicals. We don't all have to be in lockstep, but throughout the history of our faith, the church has established some essentials, which we in the United Methodist Church have turned into nonessentials. Our problem is unchecked theological pluralism. We need to help each other think theologically and embrace a robust, vibrant Wesleyan theology in the midst of a swirling culture because we often no longer know what we believe in.

As evangelical United Methodists, we are for Jesus. We believe in a risen, living, grace-giving, sin-forgiving, life-changing Jesus who accepts us as we are and transforms us into who he created us to be. We believe in the nature and authority of the Scripture as has been embraced by the majority of Christians around the world for two thousand years. We believe in a global movement of Wesleyan Jesus followers who are committed to take the life-changing message of the gospel to every people, tribe, clan, and tongue. We believe in the new birth as described in the Scripture and taught by John Wesley. We believe in holiness of heart and life—and not just a moral code or rules and regulations that must be followed to be "Christian." We believe in a thoughtful faith that warms and changes the heart and works itself out in social justice that is connected to personal holiness. We believe in the deep transformation that happens through the Holy Spirit, which enables us to perfectly love God and neighbor as we are being renewed every day.

Reform Our Systems

Although this is the least glamorous of the changes required, there simply is no need for much of our institutional bureaucracy. Other voices have called for this right-sizing of systems and structures, and even the world of business has embraced the concept of going "lean." The system and structure of our denomination was developed for a bygone era, but it continues to be propped up rather than reformed and right-sized. Furthermore, we have often organized the Holy Spirit right out of our movement.

Twenty years ago, I was surrounded by bishops and other leaders at a denominational meeting as we listened to a young man from Africa who was responsible for evangelism in one of the fastest-growing areas in United Methodism. They had no money, resources, or institutional support to help them do what they were doing. Nevertheless, the church in that area was growing exponentially.

One of the bishops asked him how he did it, and he said, "We put a church in every village and we do four things at every church: (1) we teach people to read because education is the key to their future; (2) we teach people to farm so that they can feed themselves; (3) we provide basic healthcare which is the only healthcare in the villages; and (4) we share Jesus with everybody!" They were not encumbered with a top-heavy institution that was draining the life and resources out of its churches. They had a simple, laser-focused vision and system to meet the physical and spiritual needs of their mission field. We need to reform our system for missional focus and flexibility.

In the immediate future, pastors and local church leaders are going to have to be prepared to move into what is next for our denomination. There is not a United Methodist pastor who is going to get a pass on having this conversation. If we can take these four actions, we may be graced by God to reform our denomination like Wesley did in the Church of England years ago and experience the much-needed transformation that marks the legacy of that world-changing revival.

Questions for Discussion and Reflection

1. On a scale of one to ten (one being not at all, and ten being very), how familiar are you with the current state of the United Methodist Church?

2. What are some of your concerns or fears as our denomination grapples with cultural change?

3. In a few words, how would you characterize Methodist theology? How important is our theology to you as a United Methodist?

4. Read Acts 15:36–41. In your own words, describe what happened between Paul and Barnabas. How was the church affected? What does this story teach you about conflict within Christian circles?

5. Jeff Greenway casts a vision based on four pillars of change: refocus on Jesus, reclaim the authority of Scripture, refine our theology, and reform our systems. Which of these seems more needful to you? About which do you have questions?

6. If you could dream about your local church (and how it relates to your denomination), what would you dream for it in the next ten or twenty years? What's your deepest hope for your local church?

WITNESS

Awakening Orthodoxy

Madeline Carrasco Henners

Only five short years ago I was comfortably progressive. If we were having a conversation about the future of the United Methodist Church, I might have said, "Well, as soon as the older generation is gone, we will have our church." As a clergywoman, I would also have said what we are dealing with is the civil rights movement of our time.

So what happened? What changed my mind and heart? I was working in ministry and I looked around at my circumstances and concluded: nothing is changing. We're not growing. This is not what I'm reading about the church in the Bible. Graciously, my church gave me a month's sabbatical time to study and be at home and to unplug. I thought I was going have time to rest, to take a breath. Before long, I realized the Lord had other plans in mind. I was worshipping, I was reading the Bible, I was praying, and I was earnestly saying, "Lord, fill my heart, I need more of you." As I did, I felt this weight come upon me and the Lord clearly said: "I need you in this Word, this gospel that you're reading. I need you to see what you've added that's not here."

There is no way to prepare for being humbled by the Lord. Although it was difficult, it was also awesome because God cared enough to talk with me. I began to ask God, "What is your truth? What is your truth that transcends cultures, generations, countries, or eras?" The response I got was to pursue the truth of Christ. "Seek it, go after it, and I will not forsake you," God seemed to say. "I will show you what my truth is." If we seek with all our hearts and humble ourselves or maybe are humbled by him, then we can find a truth that has implications in our current culture, but is not dictated by it.

As I was reading the Bible, I would ask myself if I actually believed the words of our Lord were true, and possible, and achievable in this life. Did I actually believe that healing—yes of the body, spirit, and soul—was possible. Wholeness, redemption, transformation, and holiness? Who or what would I give authority over my life? Who would I trust and to what extent? Was anything truly possible through God's power as Scripture says?

As I began pressing in, I had an awakening of orthodoxy—and a charismatic awakening as well. The more you believe the truth of this Word, the more it will become true in how you walk every day. The more you trust the God who loves you so much that he is pursuing you beyond your imagination, the more the longing of our hearts for this to become reality, you get to see it every day.

Too many of us have lost a sense of expectancy that God will show up and transform our lives. Because of that disposition, we do not cry out with urgency or find ourselves willing to pay a price for revival to happen within us. In Ephesians 3:19, Paul prays that we would "know this love that surpasses knowledge—that you may be filled to the measure of all the fullness of God." To be filled with the fullness of God, we have to go beyond an intellectual knowledge of the Lord and find intimacy in the presence of God. We need to hunger for more of God and seek him with all our hearts. This is where the true transformation begins. Did Jesus die on the cross so we could feel and be just a little bit better on occasion? Was it for small victory or life-changing victory? Have we settled for less than God's fullness in our lives and ministries?

If he speaks into your heart and he lovingly humbles you, don't run. Go to the Scriptures and pray, "Lord, through your Holy Spirit, reveal your truth to me, even if it's painful. I am yours."

2

When Jesus Is Lord

David Watson

For even if there are so-called gods, whether in heaven or on earth (as indeed there are many "gods" and many "lords"), yet for us there is but one God, the Father, from whom all things came and for whom we live; and there is but one Lord, Jesus Christ, through whom all things came and through whom we live.

—1 Corinthians 8:5-6

I can't tell you how many times I've heard people say, "All religions teach the same thing."

They do not.

The oldest Christian statement of faith is, "Jesus is Lord," and only Christians believe this. People of other faiths may say, "Jesus is good," or, "Jesus is wise," but not, "Jesus is Lord."

There are many "gods," Paul says, and many "lords." The world Paul lived in was intensely religious. There were Jews, who worshipped only the God of Israel, but most people in Paul's world worshipped numerous gods. The gods of the Greco-Roman world were everywhere. There were statues and paintings of gods in the household, marketplaces, and everyplace else you can think of, from palaces to public toilets. There were gods who might be especially helpful with your business, and others who might help you win over a lover. There were gods who were thought to bring health and healing, and others who might help with childbearing. Some people worshipped the Roman emperor as a god, and even the empire itself. Gods were everywhere, and they touched on every aspect of life. In the modern West, we tend to distinguish between religious and nonreligious parts of life. Such was not the case in Paul's world. Everything was religious.

Into this context came the early Christians, taking their cues from the people of Israel before them. Like their non-Christian neighbors, they saw every aspect of life as religious. Unlike their neighbors, however, they believed that one God, who came to us in Jesus, had dominion over everything—from what you ate to whom you slept with to how you spent your money. This one God, revealed to us in Jesus, is Lord of all, they said.

As Paul said, there are many so-called gods, many so-called lords. Are things so different for us today? We may, of course, choose from a bewildering array of religions, including more established ones such as Buddhism, Islam, or Christianity, and more recent additions such as new-age practices and Scientology. We may attempt to reject religion altogether. We might become atheists or one of an increasing number of "nones"—those who simply identify with no particular religious group or set of beliefs. Then there is the "spiritual but not religious" crowd consisting of people who hold deeply individualistic forms of belief, affirming a spiritual component to life but rejecting "organized religion." No doubt we could name others as well.

There are, however, contenders for the role of "god" and "lord" in our lives beyond the faith we profess. The lord of your life may be any number of things. Politics, sex, work, patriotism, sports, and physical appearance are all common idols of Western culture. No, we don't actually call them gods. We know, in reality, that they are not eternal. Rationally, we understand that they will pass away. Despite all of this, however, we give them dominion. We allow them to occupy the space in our lives where only God should be. We allow different aspects of our lives to lord over us. John Wesley wrote of Christians in his own day, "We do not, like the idolatrous heathens, worship molten or graven images. We do not bow down to the stock of a tree, to the work of our own hands. . . . But what then? We 'have set up our idols in our heart'; and to these we bow down, and worship them."[1]

Make no mistake: if Jesus is not Lord of our lives, someone or something else will be. Jesus taught, "No one can serve two masters. Either you will hate the one and love the other, or you will be devoted to the one and despise the other. You cannot serve both God and money" (Matt. 6:24). By the same token, you cannot serve God and politics. You cannot serve God and sex. You cannot serve God and work. Yes, you can participate in politics, you can have a healthy and righteous sex life, and you can strive to succeed in your work. Only one, though, may truly have dominion over your life. When the demands of politics and the demands of following Jesus come into conflict, and they inevitably will, which will you choose? When you are tempted to engage in sexual activities that are outside the bounds of Christian morality, such as viewing pornography, how will you handle this? When you are working so much that you have no time for prayer and Sabbath, will you continue to prioritize work over your relationship with Jesus? You can only have one highest priority. You can only have one lord, and of the many lords from which we may choose, only Jesus will bring us true peace, a heart in line with God's heart, and eternal life.

For Jesus to be Lord of our lives, we must offer him three things: our obedience, our trust, and our love. Anything less, and we are denying him his rightful place as our Lord.

---

1. John Wesley, Sermon 44, "Original Sin," in *First Series of Sermons (40–53)*, ed. Thomas Jackson, vol. 6 of *The Works of John Wesley*, 3rd ed. (Grand Rapids, MI: Baker Books, 1996), 60.

Obedience

We are all obedient to someone or something. In our day and time, particularly in Western culture, we like to think of ourselves as individuals, the masters of our own destiny, self-made people. These notions of our own autonomy and individuality, however, are simply fantasies. We are shaped by culture. We are influenced by family and friends. We meet people whom we emulate, perhaps without even knowing it. At times we become enamored with charismatic leaders. We fall under the influence of advertising. The question is not whether someone or something exerts authority over our lives, but who or what does so.

Giving Jesus Authority

To say that Jesus is Lord means that we are intentionally giving him authority over our lives. It means that we are committing ourselves to obeying what he taught. This is no small thing, and it certainly isn't easy. It involves far more than simply being a good person or being nice to other people. Obedience to Jesus means that we will think, speak, and act in ways that are deeply countercultural, and sometimes counterintuitive.

Let's take, for example, some of Jesus' teachings in the Sermon on the Mount. In Matthew 5:21–22, Jesus teaches, "You have heard that it was said to the people long ago, 'You shall not murder, and anyone who murders will be subject to judgment.' But I tell you that anyone who is angry with a brother or sister will be subject to judgment. . . . And anyone who says, 'You fool!' will be in danger of the fire of hell." Almost everyone will agree that committing murder is a bad idea. But getting angry with a brother or sister (i.e., another Christian)? That's a much taller order. Personally, I've been mad at plenty of people, including Christians. Name-calling, moreover, is almost a national pastime, especially on social media. We may or may not call someone a fool outright, but there are innumerable backhanded ways to insult other people.

Jesus also says, "You have heard that it was said, 'You shall not commit adultery.' But I tell you that anyone who looks at a woman lustfully has already committed adultery with her in his heart" (Matt. 5:27–28). Adultery, in Jesus' day, meant that a married woman had sex with a man who was not her husband. We would consider this a glaring double-standard, but that was the world in which Jesus lived and Matthew wrote. The principle of Jesus' teaching, however, extends both to men and to women. It is not enough simply to avoid the physical act of marital unfaithfulness. Jesus teaches that we should avoid allowing the feelings to grow within us that can lead to such acts.

Indeed, throughout the four Gospels, Jesus teaches many things, some of which seem attainable, others of which seem almost impossible. He teaches that there must be love within the community of faith (see John 13:34). He teaches that anyone who wants to become his followers must take up the cross and follow him. Those who want to save their lives will lose them, he says, and those who lose their lives for his sake, and for the sake of the gospel, will save them (see Mark 8:34–35). He teaches that those who eat his flesh and drink his blood (the Lord's Supper) will have eternal life (see John 6:54). He teaches that we must do to others as we would have them to do us (see Luke 6:31). He teaches many other things as well. As we immerse ourselves in the Scriptures, we come to know more fully what Jesus requires of us.

The Need for God's Help

If Jesus' demands often seem impossible, it is because, left to our own devices, they *are* impossible. We require God's help. Matthew 19:16–30 tells the story of a rich man who asks Jesus what good thing he must do to attain eternal life. Jesus tells him he must keep the commandments. The rich man apparently wants to do as little as possible to receive his reward, because he then asks Jesus which commandments he must obey. Jesus replies, "'You shall not murder, you shall not commit adultery, you shall not steal, you shall not give false testimony, honor your father and mother,' and 'love your neighbor as yourself'" (vv. 18-19). Well, the rich man responds, he has always kept these. Is there anything else he is lacking? Jesus answers him, "If you want to be perfect, go, sell your possessions and give to the poor, and you will have treasure in heaven. Then come, follow me" (v. 21). Jesus knows exactly where to pinpoint the weakness of the rich man, the one part of his life that was exercising dominion over him. The story does not tell us whether the rich man did as Jesus taught. It just says "he went away sad, because he had great wealth" (v. 22).

Jesus then takes the opportunity to teach his disciples: "it is easier for a camel to go through the eye of a needle than for someone who is rich to enter the kingdom of God" (v. 24). Why is this? Jesus is not teaching that wealth is inherently bad. Rather, he is pointing out the temptation that often accompanies wealth. Our possessions can become the lord of our lives, and no one can serve two masters.

The presenting issue does not have to be wealth, though. It can be status, pride, various forms of addiction, or beauty. For each of us, there are parts of our lives that may control our thoughts, words, and deeds. In such cases, we must surrender them to God. Only then will they no longer exercise dominion over our lives, and only then can we truly be obedient to Jesus.

The disciples seem to understand the breadth of Jesus' teaching. They realize that he is not simply teaching about wealth, but about anything that holds sway over our lives. They ask him, "Who then can be saved?" (v. 25). Jesus replies that with humans, it is impossible, but with God all things are possible (see v. 26). We can live in keeping with God's will only by God's help.

In "The Character of a Methodist," Wesley writes, "A Methodist is one who has 'the love of God shed abroad in his heart by the Holy Ghost given unto him;' one who 'loves the Lord his God with all his heart, and with all his soul, and with all his mind, and with all his strength.'"[2] We are able to shed the love of God abroad because—and only because—God has given us the Holy Spirit. We have within our grasp the ability to obey God, to live as holy people in harmony with a holy God. Yet we do so not by our own strength or goodness, but by the transforming, life-changing power of the Holy Spirit in our lives.

Obedience to Jesus, then, requires humility. It requires that we understand that there are strongholds in our lives, places where we cannot overcome our own desires simply by our own power. It is core to Wesleyan belief that "we are not sufficient of ourselves to help ourselves; . . . without the Spirit of God we can do nothing but add sin to sin."[3] We need God's help, and God will indeed help us to walk in obedience to Jesus if we will humble ourselves and ask. God changes our desires and molds them into the image of Jesus. We see things differently than we ever did before, and we live in a new and better way. This is called *sanctification*, and only through sanctification can we truly be obedient to Jesus and make him Lord of our lives.

Trust

The Gospel of Mark tells a story about a time when Jesus and his disciples are in a boat on the Sea of Galilee. A storm rose up, threatening to swamp the ship, but Jesus, perfectly calm, is sleeping

---

2. John Wesley, "The Character of a Methodist," in *Addresses, Essays, and Letters*, ed. Thomas Jackson, vol. 8 of *The Works of John Wesley*, 3rd ed. (Grand Rapids, MI: Baker Books, 1996), 341.
3. John Wesley, Sermon 17, "The Circumcision of the Heart," in *First Series of Sermons (1-39)*, ed. Thomas Jackson, vol. 5 of *The Works of John Wesley*, 3rd ed. (Grand Rapids, MI: Baker Books, 1996), 203-4.

soundly in the midst of the storm. In their fear of the storm the disciples wake him up and say, "Teacher, don't you care if we drown?" (4:38). Jesus awakes and commands the wind and the sea to be still. Then he asks his disciples why they were afraid. "Do you still have no faith?" (4:40).

The Greek word that we translate as "faith," *pistis*, also means trust. When Jesus asks his disciples if they still have no faith, he is asking them whether they trust him. Fear and faith here stand in opposition to one another. When Paul says that "a person is not justified by the works of the law, but by faith in Jesus Christ" (Gal. 2:16), he means not just that we should believe in Jesus, but that we should trust in Jesus. We should trust that he shows us the good life. We should trust that on the cross he has broken the power of sin over our lives. We should trust that he has conquered death. Trust in Jesus is essential if he is to be Lord of our lives.

The Good Life

There are lots of competing ideas about what the good life entails. It might involve wealth, power, and sex, or, on the other hand, simplicity, family, and fidelity. The good life, from a Christian perspective, is one lived in harmony with God's will. Jesus shows us which values lead us into keeping with God's will, and which do not. If we trust in his teachings to guide our lives, we will learn that a life lived in keeping with God's will is truly good. Jesus teaches this point using a parable about building a house on a rock or on sand (see Matthew 7:24-27).

Entrusting our lives to Jesus is like building upon a rock. Jesus' teachings provide a sure foundation for our lives. He teaches us to deal compassionately with both friends and enemies. He teaches us to give of ourselves. He teaches us to be humble and, above all, to seek God in every aspect of our lives. Imagine a life lived in this way. What a life of peace it would be! Imagine a whole world living in keeping with these teachings. What a different and wonderful world it would be!

Freedom from Sin

If you don't believe in original sin, just turn on the evening news. Sin is all around us. The world is infected with it like a chronic disease. Belief in *original* sin involves the idea that, apart from Jesus, we are necessarily under the power of sin. This is a core tenet of Wesleyan belief. We can't escape sin by ourselves. Sin makes us see the world in the wrong way, and thus we do things we shouldn't. In Romans 7:14–25, Paul describes the human condition as a cycle of sin and frustration. Even when we know the right thing to do, he says, we often don't do it. There is only one who can rescue us from this morass: "Thanks be to God, who delivers me through Jesus Christ our Lord!" (7:25). When Jesus died on the cross, he broke the vise-grip of sin on our lives. Now we can escape. Now we can live the way God wants us to live. We need only put our whole trust in Christ for our salvation. Once we do, the Holy Spirit begins to work in our lives in a new way, moving us onward toward perfect love for both God and our neighbors.

The other way in which Jesus frees us from sin, however, is by lifting off of us the guilt of sin. We have all spoken and acted in ways that are inconsistent with God's will. First John 1:8–9 teaches us: "If we claim to be without sin, we deceive ourselves and the truth is not in us. If we confess our sins, he is faithful and just and will forgive us our sins and purify us from all unrighteousness." Yes, we all sin, and we all "fall short of the glory of God" (Rom. 3:23). Jesus, however, offers us the forgiveness of our sins. That is to say, through the cross, Jesus offers us *atonement*. This is a theological term that means we are forgiven of sin and reconciled with God. Think of atonement as *at-one-ment*. We were separated from God by sin, but now we can be at one with God again.

Overcoming Death

Each of us, no matter how well we eat and how much we exercise, is going to die at some point. We are reminded of this every Ash Wednesday with the imposition of ashes upon our foreheads as we hear the words, "Remember that you are dust, and to dust you shall return" (see Genesis 3:19). The writer of Ecclesiastes teaches us, "people go to their eternal home and mourners go about the streets. . . . and the dust returns to the ground it came from, and the spirit returns to God who gave it" (12:5, 7). This work was written long before Jesus came, and the writer has no concept of the resurrection life. Thus he writes, "Meaningless! Meaningless! . . . Everything is meaningless!" (12:8).

In Christ, however, nothing is meaningless. Our whole lives, from the most mundane parts to the most extraordinary, are imbued with new meaning. It is not simply the case that, when we die, we pass away and over time are simply forgotten. Rather, although our natural bodies die, we know that because of Jesus, death is not the end. It is, in fact, just the beginning. Having died in this life, we are born into eternity. We will not all "sleep" for eternity, writes Paul, but "we will all be changed . . . When the perishable has been clothed with the imperishable, and the mortal with immortality, then the saying that is written will come true: 'Death has been swallowed up in victory.' 'Where, O death, is your victory? Where, O death, is your sting?'" (1 Cor. 15:51, 54–55).

When Jesus died on the cross, it looked to his followers like all hope was lost. In God, however, hope is never lost. After three days, God raised Jesus from the dead. The tomb was empty. Jesus is alive. His resurrection, moreover, anticipates our own resurrection. Paul calls Jesus the "firstfruits" of those who have died (see 1 Corinthians 15:23). This is an agricultural metaphor. At the time of the harvest, there would be a ceremonial gathering of the firstfruits, just a small amount of the total harvest which was dedicated to God (see Leviticus 23:9–14; Deuteronomy 26:1–10). Then, a short time later, the harvest would begin in earnest. Just as the gathering of the firstfruits precedes the harvest, so the resurrection of Jesus precedes the general resurrection. Just as Jesus was raised, we will all be raised. Wesley describes the resurrected state of those who are saved as one of perfect communion with God, an "unmixed state of holiness and happiness far superior to that which Adam enjoyed in paradise."[4] There will be no more pain, sickness, death, or sin.

Trust in our salvation in Jesus changes the way we understand the end of our mortal lives. Death is sometimes very painful, and it is certainly hard for those who are left behind. In Christ, though, we know that death is not the end. If Jesus is the Lord of our lives, we will trust him not just with this life, but with our eternal lives.

Love

"We love," says Scripture, "because [God] first loved us" (1 John 4:19). It was out of God's great love that we were brought into being. To save us from sin, God became human in Jesus Christ. Jesus taught us how to live in keeping with God's will. He healed the sick, cast out demons, and raised the dead. He died on the cross not only to free us from slavery to sin, but to give us the opportunity for eternal life. After he rose from the dead, he sent the Holy Spirit as a comforter, advocate, and teacher. God's love for us is expressed in these immeasurable acts of self-giving.

Therefore, as we return God's love, we do so in acts of self-giving. We give God our thoughts, our bodies, our money, our emotions. We do this not out of obligation or fear, but out of love. If we try to follow God, but do not do so out of love, we will have, as

---

4. John Wesley, Sermon 64, "The New Creation," in *Second Series Begun (54–86)*, ed. Thomas Jackson, vol. 6 of *The Works of John Wesley*, 3rd ed. (Grand Rapids, MI: Baker Books, 1996), 296.

Wesley put it, "the toils and not the joys of religion."[5] The gospel is the story of how God first loved us, and if we believe that story, if we allow it to shape the way we see ourselves and the world around us, how can we respond but with love?

More Than Emotions

The love of Jesus does involve our emotions, but it also involves more than that. It is an orientation of life that gives meaning to everything else we do. The things of this world constantly try to draw us away from God. They tell us that they can make us happy, that we should give them our love instead, but there is no life or joy in that lie. Augustine taught that there are things in this world that can bring us delight, but that they will only truly delight us if we understand them in relation to God. Otherwise, they will rightly turn bitter, and instead of bringing us joy they will bring unhappiness. In other words, our relationship with Jesus becomes the lens through which we see everything in our lives. The way we look at both friends and strangers, the way we think about raising children, our financial management, the way we spend our time, our daily routines—all of these become subservient to Jesus' lordship.

The Surpassing Worth of Jesus

In Philippians, Paul talks about the life he had before he came to know Christ. He had all the right credentials for a Jewish person of his day: "If someone else thinks they have reasons to put confidence in the flesh, I have more: circumcised on the eighth day, of the people of Israel, of the tribe of Benjamin, a Hebrew of Hebrews; in regard to the

---

5. John Wesley, Sermon 29, "Upon Our Lord's Sermon on the Mount, Discourse the Ninth," in *First Series of Sermons (1–39)*, ed. Thomas Jackson, vol. 5 of *The Works of John Wesley*, 3rd ed. (Grand Rapids, MI: Baker Books, 1996), 383.

law, a Pharisee; as for zeal, persecuting the church; as for righteousness based on the law, faultless" (3:4–6). Yet Paul was willing to give
up all of this for one reason: his love of Christ. "But whatever were
gains to me I now consider loss for the sake of Christ. What is more, I
consider everything a loss because of the surpassing worth of knowing
Christ Jesus my Lord, for whose sake I have lost all things. I consider
them garbage, that I may gain Christ and be found in him" (3:7–9).

How does this apply to our lives today? Ask yourself what identity
markers and accomplishments are most important to you. In my own
case, for example, I might say that I am a cradle United Methodist,
baptized and raised in our church, educated in one of our seminaries,
and ordained in our tradition. I completed my PhD at Southern
Methodist University. I have spent more hours than I can count in
meetings related to both ordination and seminary education. I've
served on the ministerial staff of a United Methodist church, I attend a
United Methodist church weekly with my family, and I even co-wrote
a book called *Key United Methodist Beliefs*. I now work in a United
Methodist seminary. I am United Methodist by heritage, formation, education, and choice. But in comparison to the surpassing
value of knowing Christ, all of this is meaningless. This heritage,
my upbringing and formation in the United Methodist Church, my
education and service to this denomination should all serve Christ,
and if they do not, then they are of no value to me as a follower of
Christ. Sometimes I forget this. Sometimes I'm better at being a
United Methodist than at being a follower of Jesus. Sometimes my
loyalties get confused. Sometimes I falter in my love for Jesus.

To whom, or what, are you most loyal? Who or what directs
your actions? Who or what motivates you? What do you spend
your money on? Your answer to these questions will help you to see
whom you love, who is lord of your life. You may have a favorite
sports team, but do you spend so much money on games and
merchandise that you cannot tithe to the church? You may support
a certain political party, but are you so loyal to this party that you

are willing to look the other way when it advocates for policies that are inconsistent with Jesus' teachings? You may love to read books or play video games, but do you spend so much time doing so that you forget to pray? It is so easy to turn our love away from Jesus, to set up idols and offer them our devotion. Yet none of these idols will ever truly satisfy. None will free us from sin. None will give us eternal life. None can ever love us the way Jesus loves us.

Worshipping Jesus

This is one reason that we worship Jesus (God the Son, along with God the Father and God the Holy Spirit). It is a way of expressing our devotion and love to him. Worship is a very serious matter in the Bible. Anyone or anything we worship other than the God of Israel who came to us in Jesus becomes an idol. The Ten Commandments forbid the making and worship of idols (see Exodus 20:2–6), yet we read again and again in the Old Testament how the people of Israel strayed from the worship of the one true God and bowed down to them. We should not be too hard on them, though. Today we simply have different idols. To commit ourselves to times of worship where we can proclaim that Jesus is Lord and offer our thanks and praise for the salvation he gives us is a way to resist the lure of idols. Through worship, we demonstrate and reinforce our devotion to our one true Lord.

Conclusion

If people called Methodist are once again to represent a mighty movement of God in North America, we will have to recover a clear sense of what it means to call Jesus "Lord." In Wesley's day, the Methodist movement stood in sharp contrast to the values, practices, and worldview of the surrounding culture. In our own day, we must again find our voice as a Christian counterculture. We will necessarily have a deeper sense of being in this world, but not of it. We will once again feel the friction of being "foreigners and exiles" (1 Pet. 2:11). To give Jesus our obedience, trust, and love will inevitably place us in tension with those who do not believe. Are we willing to live in this tension? Are we willing to experience ridicule for Jesus, to lose friends and be misunderstood by family? To say that Jesus is Lord is more than simply a doctrinal confession. It is a declaration of ultimate allegiance. May God give us the will and strength to be a peculiar people once again, to obey, trust, and love the one who is Lord of all.

Questions for Discussion and Reflection

1. Reread the Scripture that opens this chapter (1 Corinthians 8:5-6). Can you rephrase this passage in your own words?

2. What is the difference between "God" and "Lord" in this passage? Can you name an area in your life where you may not have given Christ permission to be Lord?

3. In what ways do you live out the lordship of Jesus in your own life? How would someone on the outside looking in be able to tell that, for you, Jesus is Lord?

4. Obedience to Jesus requires humility. How would you define humility? What characterizes a life of obedience rooted in humility?

5. Read 1 John 4:19. What does this passage teach us about the connection between our capacity to love and the fact of Jesus' love for us?

6. However you imagine the good life, how can you tell if you're becoming too preoccupied with it?

7. "If the people called Methodist are once again to represent a mighty movement of God in North America, we will have to recover a clear sense of what it means to call Jesus 'Lord.'" How do you envision a church in complete obedience to the lordship of Jesus?

WITNESS

Living and Relevant Church Today

Carlos Pirona

History tends to repeat itself. The times of Jesus are not so unlike the times of John Knox, William Booth, or John Wesley, whose times were not so unlike our own. Scientific breakthroughs and technological advances make us believe our generation is grandly unique and qualified to transform a society, but that is an illusion. The moral and spiritual climate today—one that places the human being at the center of all things—is much the same as when Jesus walked the earth. This climate continues to deserve our righteous and meaningful response.

Some would have us offer mere sympathy. Unfortunately, sympathy (or pity) looks at the human heart from a position of superiority and simply gives answers that satisfy for a moment, but are unable to help men and women find restoration.

Compassion, on the other hand, looks at the human being in the midst of spiritual chaos and sees men and women from a different vantage point; namely, that they are made in the image of their Creator and designed to be healed, restored, and transformed.

We are following the model of Jesus when we see people as capable of finding spiritual restoration—recipients of healing, freedom, and purpose. When Jesus saw the crowds, "he had compassion on them, because they were harassed and helpless, like sheep without a shepherd" (Matt. 9:36). The incarnate love in Jesus and his expression manifested in the painful and cruel cross challenges us to give everything—give *everything*—for the child, young man, woman, man, family, businessman, immigrant, professional, literate or not, et cetera.

It is the gospel of the kingdom and its manifestations with power and authority in the person of Jesus Christ that marked a "before" and "after" in human history. Filled with the Holy Spirit, the disciples of Jesus did not go unnoticed in the streets and neighboring towns.

If we want to transform cities and nations, we must hear again the message of Jesus. It is the message that every person on earth receives an expression of his unconditional love. This message requires courageous representatives who—leaving comfort, complacency, and security—become reformers through the power of the Holy Spirit to communicate a fresh and relevant word to our culture.

John Wesley was responsive to the call of God to address his culture in his time. He was responsible for a passionate evangelistic movement that shook the structures of all spheres of society in his era through a message centered on a holy, loving, and just God. This is our heritage as Wesleyans. We are responsible for carrying forth what we have received and mobilizing believers and engaging them fully in every arena through the love and grace of a just God.

Ministering within my own native Venezuela, I know how important it is that we provide the spiritual tools and the theological foundations to church leaders, especially if we are serious about reaching the high population of young people who are looking for purpose and truth and meaning in their lives. This young generation is learning from us how to mobilize in the midst of severe political, economic, and social crises, and innovate for the kingdom of God.

The next generation will not be satisfied with staying in their seats, remaining inactive within the walls of beautiful buildings. The next generation longs to be fully engaged in their spheres of influence with the Great Commission within a Wesleyan spirit. They are seeking training so they can plant indigenous churches; intentionally reach the lost; and introduce the Source of life, hope, and salvation in each community in which they serve. This is our driving passion at the Wesleyan Seminary of Venezuela. It is our commitment to see each person we influence to find the power of the Holy Spirit, maintain an intimacy with the Father, and manifest real and visible fruits through evangelism and discipleship. We long for a generation equipped with a robust and healthy teaching of the faith so we see an abundant harvest that does not stop in Venezuela but runs through the world.

To God be the glory!

3

Faithfully Engaging the Scriptures

Chris Ritter

All Scripture is God-breathed and is useful for teaching, rebuking, correcting and training in righteousness, so that the servant of God may be thoroughly equipped for every good work.

—2 Timothy 3:16-17

I swear . . . on a stack of Bibles!" That was the most binding vow that a kid could take on the playgrounds of my childhood. Ignorant of what Scriptures actually had to say about swearing, our logic flowed like this: if taking vows on one Bible was good enough to satisfy a judge, then swearing on a pile of them was even better.

Stacked or single, the Bible stands as a symbol for the highest ideals of truth. In the United States, our presidents do not vow to defend the Constitution by placing their hands on the Constitution. They place their hands on the Bible.

The shallow compliments our increasingly secular culture still pays to the Bible are the residue of the respect and honor the church has paid the Scriptures over the centuries. The Bible is the church's book (or, more precisely, our library). These are the texts we read, love, study, proclaim, wrestle with, and seek to order our lives around. They tell a sweeping epic of salvation that includes us in the story. We use many books, but the Bible is our canon, our measuring stick, for truth. It tells us where we come from, why we are here, how we should live, and where we are headed. And the canon is closed; we do not add to or take away. Yard sticks are never made of elastic.

The Scripture holds authority in our lives because God does. Jesus Christ is Lord and our response to his lordship is faith exercised in joyful obedience. The Bible is not just a book *about* God; it is *from* God. It is our Creator's intentional and gracious self-revelation, a divine autobiography. The inspiration of the Holy Spirit was deeply involved in the varied processes that brought the Scriptures to us.

In another sense, the Bible is 100-percent human. These texts didn't fall to earth from heaven in a leather binding. They came over a long period of time through kings, priests, prophets, chroniclers, and apostles. Each one was a saint *and* a sinner. Each had their own historical reality and reasons for writing. None of them were likely aware that they were writing the Bible. Yet, through people scattered over thousands of years and thousands of miles, the Holy Spirit brought us the testaments of God's faithful love. Many different authors dipped their quills to write, but God is the grand architect behind it all.

The Good Book is a tough book. When I challenged a congregation I served to read through the Bible in a year, a friend of mine began reading the Bible for the first time in her life. About a month in, she confronted me in total exasperation: "I thought this was a book about good people doing good things. It's not!"

I explained, "No, it is not a book about good people. It is about sinful people being pursued by a holy God." I told her I could relate to her vexation. Sometimes the Bible comforts me, but many times it has made me very uncomfortable. This is true of the parts I don't understand and the parts I do. You don't have to spend a long time in the Bible to realize you are reading texts from a reality very different from our own. Yet, because it is all about relationships, it remains surprisingly relevant—even miraculously relevant.

Above all, the Bible is the place where we meet Jesus. John's Gospel opens with the declaration that Jesus is the Word made flesh. To the Pharisees, Jesus said, "You study the Scriptures diligently because you think that in them you have eternal life. These are the very Scriptures that testify about me, yet you refuse to come to me to have life" (John 5:39–40). It is possible to read the Bible very seriously and studiously, and yet miss the forest for the trees. The best reason to study Scripture is to meet Jesus. The Bible is an owner's manual for a faithful walk with Jesus.

Discovering the Word

I first met Sam when our church held a block party in his neighborhood a few years ago. We grilled hot dogs and made balloon animals on a sunny Saturday afternoon while a band played upbeat songs of praise. I noticed Sam and how deeply engaged in conversation he was with one of our men. Even from a distance, it was obvious to me that he was a spiritual seeker.

To our delight, our new friend showed up for worship the next day. He would later tell me that coming into our sanctuary for the first time felt like coming home. But, boy, did he have questions! "What is a Methodist? What do you believe? What about the Virgin Mary?" Sam had been raised as a Roman Catholic in Puerto Rico. Now middle-aged, he had lately been taking regular visits from Jehovah's Witnesses. They caused him to further doubt the faith of his childhood, but he was not ready to join the Kingdom Hall. He didn't know what to believe.

Lots of different people in our church poured into Sam's thirsty soul. He seemed relieved that we didn't seem too eager to make him a Methodist. We wanted to introduce him to the God of the Scriptures and the joy of salvation through Jesus Christ. Sam soon started reading and carrying a Bible. But what really fed his soul was talking about the Word with others. A Bible class on Sunday mornings kept him on the edge of his seat. He caused a scene one morning when the teacher dismissed one of his questions by telling him he would get back to him later. Sam protested: "No! I want answers now!"

Sam was without a driver's license for a while and was happy for me to pick him up early for church, even though we arrived two hours before Sunday school. He would sit in an empty classroom and read. The first book of the Bible he discovered was Matthew. While working through this Gospel, he fell in love with Jesus.

Sam is now a leader in our church. He recently told me, "I find myself doing things that I never thought I would do, like talk to strangers about Jesus." I asked Sam to summarize the change that has happened in his life. He said, "I know the true Word of God. Jesus is the Word."

Wesleyans and the Word

As the spiritual heirs of John Wesley, we are Bible people. Wesley read and wrote on an amazingly wide range of topics. Yet, he called himself a "man of one book." He even went so far as to call himself a "Bible bigot." Wesley's prejudice was in favor of what the Scriptures said and how they said it: "I follow it in all things, great and small," he confessed. Wesley's ministry methods, he admitted, were "irregular." It is important to note, however, that he never aspired to create some sort of new theology. He saw himself as proclaiming the good, old truth of the apostles and early church as recorded in Scripture.

For Wesley, the main subject of the Bible is not science, literature, or history, but salvation. This is seen clearly in a famous quote from the preface of his collected sermons:

> I want to know one thing—the way to heaven; how to land safe on that happy shore. God himself has condescended to teach me the way. For this very end He came from heaven. He hath written it down in a book. O give me that book! At any price, give me the book of God! I have it: here is knowledge enough for me. Let me be *homo unius libri* [a man of

one book]. Here then I am, far from the busy ways of men. I sit down alone; only God is here. In His presence I open, I read His book; for this end, to find the way to heaven.[1]

In his sermon "On Corrupting the Word of God," Wesley warned against the various ways Scripture is often abused. He remarked that "scarce ever was any erroneous opinion either invented or received, but Scripture was quoted to defend it."[2] As with Jesus in the wilderness, Satan can quote Scripture as well as anyone (see Luke 4:9–12). Wesley warned against rejecting those parts of the Bible that seem rough or that are critical of the common practices of our culture. These might be the words we need to hear the most.

Reading the Bible Faithfully

Those seeking God through the grace of Jesus Christ and in the power of the Holy Spirit will have a deep desire to read the Bible well. This means reading regularly with our hearts laid open for God to speak to us, shape us, heal us, and correct us. We ask the Holy Spirit who inspired the text to bring it to life for us. In this way, the Bible becomes "alive and active. Sharper than any double-edged sword . . . [judging] the thoughts and attitudes of the heart" (Heb. 4:12).

One discussion I find decidedly unhelpful is whether or not the Bible should be taken literally. I encounter folks who find it convenient to say, "I love the Bible. I just don't take it literally." If "literal" means taking words at their most basic meaning without metaphor or allegory, no one reads the Bible this way. Scripture is chock-full of metaphors, allegories, and figures of speech. We have

---

1. Preface from John Knox, *John Wesley's 52 Standard Sermons: An Annotated Summary* (Eugene, OR: Wipf & Stock, 2017), vi.
2. *The Works of the Reverend John Wesley, A.M.* Volume 2 (New York: J. Emory and B. Waugh, 1831), 504.

poems, psalms, prophecies, and parables that are meant to convey a meaning beyond their literal meaning.

Consider Ecclesiastes 10:2: "The heart of the wise inclines to the right, but the heart of the fool to the left." Should I have an echocardiogram to see which direction my cardiac organ is leaning? No. "Heart" is a metaphor for the deepest place from which we each determine, deliberate, and decide. To take this passage literally would be to profoundly misinterpret it. Francis Schaeffer, the twentieth-century Christian apologist, said that he never refers to the "literal view" of Scripture because "that is literally not accurate."[3]

We need to talk, instead, about a *faithful* reading of the Bible. This means using all the tools at our disposal to understand what the writers were saying to their original audience and employing time-tested methods of interpretation to determine how it applies to our lives. We give attention to the historic and literary context. We note the genre. We seek to understand the literary devices that the author employs.

Being divinely inspired, the entirety of Scripture is authoritative for Christian faith and practice. It is *all* God's Word. When there are seeming conflicts, we harmonize specific passages with what Wesley called "the whole tenor of Scripture." Christians have never weighed all Scripture equally in terms of their direct application to the Christian life. For two thousand years we have been distinguishing between ceremonial and dietary laws that are not directly binding upon Christians and moral Old Testament laws that are. But all Scripture has value. We understand the Hebrew Scriptures through the lens of the New Covenant brought by the life, death, and resurrection of Jesus.

Finally, we read the Bible in the company of the church. We attend Bible studies and hear sermons. We consult with one another on the meaning and application of the texts. It takes humility for me

---

3. See https://www.thegospelcoalition.org/article/fact-checker-do-faithful-christians -take-the-bible-literally.

to accept that I have likely never had an original thought about any passage of Scripture I have ever read. (If I did, it was almost certainly wrong.) Every passage in the Bible has been studied and commented upon more than any other writing in human history. We stand in a long line of faithful readers who have found in Scripture a grand narrative that stretches from Genesis to Revelation. There is a rich and certain inheritance we have received from the saints who have gone before us. This is the treasure of orthodoxy.

Biblical Authority Challenged

The Bible opens with creation and the fall. Adam had been placed in Eden to bless and to be blessed. Eve was taken from his side as a partner to enjoy and promulgate the riches of God's creation. The tree of life stood in the center of the garden from which they could freely eat and live forever. They walked and talked with God in the cool of the evening.

When relationship is strong, rules are few. In fact, God only placed one gracious limit on the couple. They were not to eat the fruit of the tree of the knowledge of good and evil that stood alongside the tree of life in the center of their enormous botanical home. If they did, they would surely die. We don't know how long Adam and Eve lived in paradise enjoying full communion with their Creator and each other. But we are told how it all ended: the serpent asked, "Did God really say, 'You must not eat from any tree in the garden'?" (Gen. 3:1).

The whispered question immediately prompted Eve's clarification. God said they could eat from any of the trees, except the one. The serpent then suggested that things would go better for them if they skirted God's command. Perhaps God was looking out for his own interests instead of theirs. A posture of mistrust was suggested, and Adam and Eve bit. Sin led to exile and exile led to death. And it all started with, "Did God really say?"

I love the United Methodist Church. I was raised in the back pew of Cache Chapel United Methodist Church. I accepted Christ as my Savior and a call to ministry at a United Methodist camp. I attended United Methodist seminaries. It grieves me deeply to say that United Methodism is in trouble. While we are growing in Africa and other parts of the world, we have a fifty-year unbroken pattern of numerical decline in the United States. It would be one thing if we were shrinking because we offered a compelling demonstration of the gospel that our culture rejected. The truth is that we are becoming indistinguishable from the larger culture in terms of our values. The salt is losing its savor. When this happens, the church has nothing to offer that can't be found elsewhere. Inside the church, divisions run deep over the very topics that should be uniting us. Schism in terms of belief and practice is quickly becoming formalized. At the root of these woes is the question: "Did God really say?"

The problems are not new. You can look back at previous generations and find our fiery, flourishing, frontier faith busily building universities, seminaries, hospitals, boards, and agencies as we embraced our status as arguably the most influential Protestant denomination in a young, Protestant nation. The ranks of the clergy became professionalized, taking us away from our lay-led roots. It was natural for Methodists to embrace higher education because John Wesley himself was an Oxford scholar and so personally passionate about learning. New waves of humanist thought, however, were hitting universities and calling into question the basic tenets of the church that sponsored them.

One response within a certain sector of the church was to accept the critique that the Bible was little more than an anthology of literature about God—inspired only in the way a poem might be inspired by a beautiful sunset. Some Methodists sought to carve out a future for our beloved old religion by partnering with those with a secular humanist social vision. Perhaps the church could busy itself transforming society apart from the supernatural claims of our faith.

Another response in some quarters of the church was Fundamentalism. This was an effort to defend the accuracy of Scripture using modern lenses. (Never mind that the Bible predates our understanding of science by hundreds or thousands of years.) In the end, both approaches proved wooden and misdirected. World wars demonstrated that human progress would only help us kill each other more efficiently apart from a change in the human heart. (The old Christian doctrine of Original Sin proved quite durable.) The Fundamentalist lens, where accepted, placed the church in a defensive posture instead of leaning us into the culture we are called to reach.

Disagreements about the Bible caused Methodists to limp into the heart of the twentieth century instead of march. In the midst of this theological malaise, denominations began to merge with one another. While the ecumenical movement had the noblest of ideals, it often seemed to be seeking unity based only on the lower common denominator of belief. Methodists went through two major mergers in 1939 and 1968. Each one yielded a murkier understanding of what we stand for and what we actually believe. The 1968 merger that formed the United Methodist Church placed Scripture alongside three other authorities: reason, tradition, and experience.

When the Bible takes a diminished place in the life of the church, we are "tossed back and forth by the waves, and blown here and there by every wind of teaching and by the cunning and craftiness of people in their deceitful scheming" (Eph. 4:14). In the United Methodist Church and our predecessors, this can be seen in the church's flirtations with Communism and eugenics in the 1920s and 1930s. It can be seen in theological education that turned out clergy less grounded in the Christian faith than when they entered. It can be seen in the ways that church has been made the servant of American political ideologies. It can be seen when a United

Methodist bishop publicly denies the virgin birth and bodily resurrection of Jesus.

Morality, Human Sexuality, and the Bible

Recent battles in the United Methodist Church have focused on Christian practice rather than doctrine. But once again the interpretation of Scripture is at the forefront. At its most basic level, the claim is made that taking the Bible at face value might cause us, in some cases, to be bad people.

One set of ethical concerns relates to the way Christians respond to changes in our culture related to human sexuality and marriage. This conversation has been heating up against the backdrop of forty years of ethical instruction in the mainline churches centered around the word *inclusion*. We all know that Jesus abolished the dividing line between Jew and Gentile. In his earthly ministry, he welcomed outsiders on many occasions. For a large number of Methodists, being inclusive, accepting, and welcoming has become the very heart of Christian morality and the standard by which all other ethical matters are viewed.

Standing in the way of this oversimplified understanding of Christian ethics is a fair amount of the New Testament. We have the ethical teachings of Jesus that do not fit under the category of inclusion. Some of the things that Jesus said were actually quite exclusive! We also have the epistles that define boundaries for the Christian life. Using inclusion as the primary grid through which to understand Christian ethics leaves us begging the question: "Include into what?" If we are including people into a life of Christian discipleship, then following Jesus means taking up a cross, not just laying down a welcome mat.

To negotiate these tensions, some would sift through the texts to separate the wheat from the chaff. I have clergy colleagues who will say before the public reading of Scripture, "Listen *for* the Word of God," instead of, "Listen *to* the Word of God." The implication is that the Word of God might be in there somewhere if we are clever enough to find it. The Bible and the Word of God are overlapping but discernably distinct, according to this view. Notable figures in United Methodism have written that the biblical passages should be sorted into different bins: those that reflect the will of God for all time, those that once reflected the will of God but do so no longer, and ones that never reflected God's will. I call this sifting and sorting "biblical revisionism." It is a tactic to use when the ethics of the Bible don't match up to the ethics we feel are the ideal.

During a recent conversation, a colleague of mine claimed that classic methods of biblical interpretation that take the Bible at face value have historically been stumbling blocks to advancements in the church—advancements that we now all agree are good things. He was speaking of female ordination, the rejection of slavery, and welcoming divorced persons into roles of church leadership. This is a significant claim that I have heard repeated in various contexts. It is a charge that deserves a response.

The practice of slavery was defeated by those with a high biblical view, not biblical revisionists. While there were certainly New Testament Scriptures used to legitimize the practice of slavery, discerning Christians understood that the slave/master relationship cited in the New Testament was a very different social arrangement than the chattel slavery that permeated North America. Biblical texts encouraging Christian submission were being co-opted by those with entrenched economic interests in owning, buying, and selling other humans. Outside those profiting from slavery, the church rejected the slave trade as a profound contradiction of the gospel. John Wesley denounced slavery as the "sum of all villainies."[4] The more Americans embraced the gospel, the more likely they were to favor

---

4. John Wesley letter to William Wilberforce, February 24, 1791. http://www
.christianitytoday.com/history/issues/issue-2/wesley-to-wilberforce.html.

abolition. Evangelical renewal in the Second Great Awakening (with its strident insistence on biblical holiness) was one of the forces that brought the issue to a head in nineteenth-century America.

Similarly, the doors were opened for women in ministry by people with the high, classic view of Scripture. While the United Methodist Church recently celebrated sixty years of female ordination, the Assemblies of God (a more conservative Pentecostal denomination) celebrated their eighty-first anniversary of the same. The Church of the Nazarene, a more conservative church in the Wesleyan family, opened ordination to women two generations before we did. The Salvation Army, another Wesleyan group, had female ordination from its start in 1865. What won the day was the positive command in Scripture for Christian women to proclaim the gospel paired with cultural realities that made this possible in a professional capacity. Biblical revisionism had nothing to do with it. To be sure, some churches using the tools of classic Christian interpretation continue to exclude women from ordained ministry. But within our Methodist history, women's ordination proves that rejecting the authority of certain scriptures is not essential to get there.

Of course, the reason for this whole discussion lately is that some in the church want to match our culture's acceptance of homosexual practice with same-sex weddings in the church. The biblical gymnastics required for this take us well beyond the process of weighing scriptures with Scripture. The whole basis for the New Testament sexual ethic would be brought into question in order to allow such an accommodation. Beyond the six unanimous prohibitions of homosexual practice found in the Old and New Testaments, we have the positive vision of human sexuality and marriage described by Jesus in Matthew 19, which same-sex pairings contradict. When Jesus was asked about technicalities in the marriage laws of his day, he pointed people back to God's original design in Genesis 2. The Bible starts with a wedding in Genesis and ends with a wedding in Revelation. Marriage bears tremendous theological weight in Scripture.[5]

At the same time, one will legitimately ask: Didn't we already do revision on a similar scale when we accepted the reality of divorce in the church, including divorced clergy? After all, Jesus himself offered some fairly comprehensive rejections of divorce in the same passage referenced above. If we can do that for divorced people, why can't we do the same to allow same-sex marriage?

In the case of divorce, those of us who allow for remarriage continue to agree with the New Testament witness. Divorce is sin because vows made before God are broken in contradiction to Jesus' direct command. If churches were asked to perform "divorce blessings," I imagine that few would. Different denominations weigh the scriptural evidence to decide whether divorce, given its universal negative, is something from which one can morally recover. What we should not do is claim that what Jesus said about divorce no longer reflects God's will.

When it comes to the ethical concerns of the church, biblical revisionists are taking undue credit for decisions the church has made using the classical tools of biblical interpretation. In fact, I cannot think of a single example of biblical revisionism helpfully reforming the church, blessing a broken world, liberating the oppressed, or redeeming the lost.

Human sexuality debates will continue in the church for decades to come. I hope that we can respond with love, compassion, humility, and Christian concern. And I sincerely hope that we do so without "selling the farm," compromising on the authority of Scripture. The early church flourished in a Roman culture where the sexual and moral values were very different

---

5. For a much more complete treatment of this complex subject, see *The Moral Vision of the New Testament: A Contemporary Introduction to New Testament Ethics* by Richard B. Hays.

than the ones in Scripture. They stuck to the lordship of Jesus and long outlived the empire that persecuted them. Today we name our children Peter and Mary and our dogs Nero and Caesar. My gut tells me that our culture desperately needs an alternative voice. A faithful church might prove to be the only haven for the countless broken refugees that will one day flee the shattered promises of the sexual revolution.

Conclusion

The God of the Bible is a redeeming God. There are indications of a grand theological recovery among Methodists. While we are declining in the United States, we are growing like gangbusters in the Global South. There is a new crop of theological minds that are calling United Methodists into the riches of orthodoxy as we wake from a period of theological amnesia. Signs are everywhere that the Holy Spirit is at work. A vital part of the recovery will be a recommitment to the Scripture as God's holy, inspired, and life-changing Word. This is not just an opinion to hold, but a conviction that will propel us forward in mission and ministry. Reclaiming the centrality of Scripture goes hand in hand with resurgence in prayer, evangelism, and service in the power of the Holy Spirit.

Having a strong statement affirming the place of the Bible in the church is crucial. It is even more important for us to demonstrate that with our lives. Join with me in opening the Bible every day with an eye toward knowing God's will for your life. When we read the Bible with an open heart and yielded life, we are breathing in what the Holy Spirit breathed out. Find a few other people willing to read and live by Scripture with you. All great moves of God started in this very manner—including Methodism.

Questions for Discussion and Reflection

1. Have you ever read the whole Bible?
2. Has your experience with Scripture grown over the years? If so, how?
3. What is one way in which the Holy Spirit has used Scripture to challenge you in your own spiritual growth?
4. What is your experience with the ways the authority of Scripture has been proclaimed by pastors? What have you learned about Scripture from the sermons you've heard?
5. Read Hebrews 4:12. What do we learn about the Scriptures from this verse?
6. Have you experienced anyone misusing the Bible to justify his or her own opinions? Have you ever used Scripture to justify your own perspective?
7. What is something in the Bible you want to understand better?
8. The future Methodism must be unified in its commitment to the authority of Scripture. What is your hope for how the Bible will be used among Methodists?

WITNESS

Committed to Scripture

Debo Onabanjo

I was privileged to have been born into a strong Christian family back in Lagos, Nigeria. My father was a fully accredited lay preacher of the Methodist Church Nigeria. As a United Methodist clergy person serving in the United States, I am thankful for our common Wesleyan heritage.

If someone were to ask me why I am a Christian, I would simply say it is because of my firm conviction in the doctrine of the triune God and that Jesus Christ is truly the way, the truth, and the life, and that no one comes to the Father except through him (see John 14:6). I have chosen to live out those faith convictions as a United Methodist.

Long before Christianity was introduced in Africa, idol worship was prevalent; however, many Africans, especially in the south-western part of Nigeria, were quick to embrace Christianity when they heard the gospel. In fact, Methodism was the first denomination to establish roots in Nigeria in 1842, and it remains a very vibrant denomination to this day. Africans were quick to embrace the Bible as the written Word of God. We believe it is truly inspired by God and cannot be altered.

While teaching a confirmation class recently at the church I am privileged to pastor, I reiterated to the students that one of the core foundational teachings of United Methodists through the years is believing that the Bible is the authoritative Word of God and that Jesus was both divine and human. This is one of the questions the students are asked at their confirmation: "Do you receive and profess the Christian faith as contained in the Scriptures of the Old and New Testaments?" While my students honestly answered, "yes," I have come to the sad realization that not all professing United

Methodists—including clergy and laity—currently accept the Bible as sufficiently authoritative for our salvation. Many do not even have a biblical worldview, according to recent surveys.

Our Doctrinal Standards affirm: "The Holy Scriptures containeth all things necessary to salvation, so that whatsoever is not read therein, nor may be proved thereby, is not to be required of any man that it should be believed as an article of faith, or be thought requisite or necessary to salvation."[6]

We are taught to embrace the teachings of Scripture and called to live in faithful adherence to the moral laws we're taught in the Bible. While the founder of Methodism, John Wesley, was widely read, he placed Scripture over and above all other books with his well-known statement, "Let me be *homo unius libri*"—a man of one book.

This commitment to Scripture is at the heart of our mandate: "to reform the nation, particularly the church; and to spread scriptural holiness over the land."[7] This has been our charge from our earliest days as a movement; it has not changed and will never change.

Just like our contemporary time, eighteenth-century England—when the Wesleyan revival broke out—was also the age of political correctness and business as usual. We live now in a similar moral environment, and more than ever before the time has come for the *next* Wesleyan revival that will proclaim boldly and courageously scriptural holiness and orthodox evangelical values throughout the land.

Our General Rules as Methodists contained in our *Book of Discipline* are clearly reflective of what we "are taught of God to observe, even in his written word, which is the *only* rule, and the sufficient rule, both of our faith and practice."[8] God will not lower

---

6. Article V in *The Book of Discipline of the United Methodist Church 2016* (Nashville, TN: The United Methodist Publishing House, 2016), 66.
7. Ibid., 12.
8. Ibid., 104, emphasis mine.

his standard for anyone, even for those he loved enough to send his beloved Son to die for. I am a Christian and a United Methodist because I believe "all Scripture is God-breathed and is useful for teaching, rebuking, correcting and training in righteousness, so that the servant of God may be thoroughly equipped for every good work" (2 Tim. 3:16–17).

When the Holy Spirit Comes with Fire

Carolyn Moore

The prayer for the Holy Spirit is a plea for the Spirit's all-embracing presence. The Spirit is more than just one of God's gifts among others. The Holy Spirit is the unrestricted presence of God in which our life wakes up, becomes wholly and entirely living, and is endowed with the energies of life.

—Jurgen Moltman

How does a log catch fire? Have you ever stopped to wonder? We drop a match into a pile of wood, and perhaps with a little help from lighter fluid or kindling, fire happens. From the outside looking in, it seems a simple and instantaneous process but there is so much more going on than meets the eye.

For wood to catch or ignite, it must heat to a temperature of between 300 and 580 degrees Fahrenheit. Assuming the log starts at room temperature, that's quite a leap! And the bigger the piece of wood, the longer it takes to heat to a combustible temperature. Likewise, the wetter the wood, the more heat it takes to evaporate the water inside and dry the wood so it can begin to heat up.

As with wood, so with people. Evan Roberts was the evangelist whose preaching sparked the 1904–1905 Welsh revival, the most widespread Christian awakening in Wales in the twentieth century. He described the months and years leading up to the moment when God set his soul ablaze. Roberts had been attending prayer meetings daily and had others praying for him as well. After years of preparation, he could sense his spiritual temperature rising. Of that season Roberts wrote, "I have only to wait for the fire. I have built the altar, and laid the wood in order, and have prepared the offering; I have only to wait for the fire."[1]

Waiting for the fire is an act of faith, but we are impatient people. We want the fire to happen in a moment and we pray for revival as if, with a little lighter fluid or kindling, we can create a blaze at our bidding. Of course, with God all things are possible; but, while supernatural things sometimes happen instantaneously, they more often happen over time. For those of us who are Methodist, this is a great assurance. After all, this is the very thing that makes us Methodist in the first place. It is our emphasis on the *process* of spiritual growth. This was how the first Holy Club—those students who gathered together under John Wesley's leadership to spur one another on toward holiness—operated. They believed that in the process of maturity, there is a season of heating up, of spiritual preparation. All that dampens our spirits—sin, circumstances, self—has to burn off before there is enough heat to catch. Try to light a wet log and you'll end up frustrated. Try to start a spiritual fire before the heat is there to sustain it, and you'll end up frustrated at best, burned at worst.

After the resurrection, Jesus met with his followers more than once. He dealt with their doubt, displayed his love for them, and commissioned them for resurrection-level ministry. But he also warned them not to get ahead of the Holy Spirit. Jesus told his followers, "*Stay here . . .* until the Holy Spirit comes and fills you with power from heaven" (Luke 24:49 NLT, emphasis mine).

---

1. The Revival Library. "Evan Roberts Testimony: 1878–1951" http://www
.revival-library.org/index.php/pensketches-menu/evangelical-revivalists/roberts
-evan-his-own-testimony. See also S. B. Shaw, *The Great Revival in Wales*. First
published in 1905. This edition 2012, Jawbone Digital Publishers.

In other words, allow time for the wood to heat up before you go starting fires. Wait for the Lord, and let the waiting do its work of sanctification so that when the Lord is ready to drop the match, the fire will catch.

Why Do We Need the Holy Spirit?

I was raised in a typical United Methodist congregation. Our worship was traditional, and our community was typically respectful in worship—notably nondemonstrative. When I was a teenager, a man in our congregation, a well-known physician with a reputation for being rather gruff, testified to having been filled with the Holy Spirit. That claim was followed by a remarkable transformation. He went from being hard to get along with to being one of the gentlest, most loving men in our church. He worshipped expressively, as one in love. He gave his testimony often. I especially remember his prayers, which reflected a warm and intimate relationship with God. Those prayers made a huge impression upon me since I hadn't witnessed anything like that in our church before.

Other than that physician, I don't remember much talk about the Holy Spirit in our church. It wasn't until I grew up, had a spiritual encounter of my own, and went to seminary that I discovered my deficit. Of course, this kind of malnourished spiritual feeding isn't the sole property of one denomination. A friend who was raised in the Pentecostal tradition tells of a similar experience with her mother. It was after her mother's death, actually, that she and her sister had a conversation about their mother's spiritual condition. Her sister told her she'd talked with their mother about the Holy Spirit, and as she put it, "Momma said she had never seen the need for it."

As sad as that must have made my friend, she says it also made a lot of things make sense. "Momma was a worrywart," she said. "She would pray over finances or health or any situation but as soon as she said 'amen,' she would begin to fret and worry. And it finally made sense to me. She had no power in her life! She didn't know she could take authority. She didn't have the peace that comes with being filled with the Holy Spirit. . . . I cannot imagine my life without the leading, guiding power of the Holy Spirit. Momma missed out on so much!"

I wonder how many of us who have grown up in the church have somehow missed out on the deeper things of God for the lack of good teaching and encouragement. How many of us have been uninspired, unmoved? How many of us have stacked the wood, added the kindling, but never struck the match?

Perhaps the apostle Paul was thinking of people like me or my friend's mother when he wrote to his friends, "I pray that you, being rooted and established in love, may have power, together with all the Lord's holy people, to grasp how wide and long and high and deep is the love of Christ, and to know this love that surpasses knowledge—that you may be filled to the measure of all the fullness of God" (Eph. 3:17-19).

Oh, to know that love! Oh, to be filled to the measure of all the fullness of God! That is an audacious prayer. That is a life-transforming prayer. Our United Methodist churches would take on a completely different tenor and tone if we opened every service, every board meeting, every Annual Conference gathering, and every General Conference with that plea to God.

The Methodist movement has lost touch with the powerful work of the Holy Spirit, and that is something we need to own and grieve.

How We Lost the Holy Spirit

There are many reasons. As in my circumstance, many Christians have grown up in churches where there never was an informative teaching on the person and work of the Holy Spirit. Some Christians are fearful that the Holy Spirit only works through loud and demonstrative personalities, ignoring those with a more low-key disposition. Regrettably, other Christians have been in congregations that suffered a dramatic split or division regarding someone's understanding of the Holy Spirit.

Some Christians have been tempted to buy into the false belief that the work of the Holy Spirit is an individualistic experience attached to individual giftedness. Still others attempt to pigeonhole the power and work of the Holy Spirit strictly to signs, wonders, and gifts of his presence. And then there are those who deny that signs and wonders occur today through the Holy Spirit.

Twentieth-century Methodism was strongly affected by theological currents that downplayed, or even outright rejected, God's direct and dramatic work in the lives of men and women. The miracles of the Bible were demythologized. God, it was said, would not or could not act in the miraculous ways we see in the Bible. The virginal conception of Christ was a myth adapted from other religions. The feeding of the five thousand never actually happened, but teaches us how to share. The resurrection of Jesus is a metaphor for the ongoing power of Jesus' message. This vision of God has not sustained the church. It has not proved compelling because it is not truthful. It did, however, form churchgoers who had little expectation that God would actually show up in their lives in any meaningful way.

Make no mistake about it, Methodism was launched as a Holy Spirit–infused global renewal movement. Unlike our friends in Pentecostal denominations, we can't point to a singular gift like speaking in tongues as the focus of the Methodist revival. It was not prosperity, or any other sign of physical abundance. To the contrary, Methodist spirituality draws on the vast variety of spiritual disciplines, engaging them in the context of community. Methodism invites the Holy Spirit to lodge within us (the temple of the Spirit) in order to raise up out of the messiness of a human life a fiery, dynamic, fully alive faith that transforms the spiritual atmosphere both within and around us.

If we're going to talk about the Holy Spirit—some of us for the first time—perhaps this analogy of how a fire catches is helpful. Think of the wood as us, our souls or our spiritual lives before God. The kindling, then, would be the practices that heat up the wood—things like worship, Bible reading, caring for the needy, prayer, group study, anything that helps us to grow in our understanding of God. And the match? Well, that is the Holy Spirit.

What Wesleyans Believe about the Holy Spirit

"Do not leave Jerusalem, but wait for the gift my Father promised, which you have heard me speak about. For John baptized with water, but in a few days you will be baptized with the Holy Spirit" (Acts 1:4–5). In speaking to his disciples, what Jesus knows is that it is the Holy Spirit who makes the rest of the story of God make sense. He reveals truth and makes it accessible to those who pursue it. He ignites the spiritual fires. He gives the process of spiritual formation its power. Without the wind of the Spirit at their backs, those first followers of Jesus would not have had the power to share the good news with a waiting world.

What did the Holy Spirit offer the disciples that they didn't already have? *Power*. In Matthew and Acts, we read that both power and authority to share the story come from God. It is not something we generate on our own. One of the Holy Spirit's primary jobs is to teach us the truth of Christ then give us power to share the story. "You will receive power when the Holy Spirit comes on you," Jesus told his followers, "and you will be my witnesses in Jerusalem, and in all Judea and Samaria, and to the ends of the earth" (Acts 1:8). The Holy Spirit is given to God's people so they can share the gospel with power. "As the Father has sent me, I am sending you," Jesus said. "Receive the Holy Spirit" (John 20:21–22).

Without the Holy Spirit's power, all our actions are limited by our fallen humanity. It is his power that allows us to commune with the Father intimately, live for God abundantly, love people supernaturally, and share the story confidently.

The Holy Spirit Is the Third Person of the Trinity

It is important to remember that Methodists seek balance in our love of God the Father, Son, and Holy Spirit. We are faithful Trinitarians. We honor our Creator as we live the teachings of Jesus and abide intimately with God through the Holy Spirit.

One of the more obvious factors leading to our decline as a denomination is how we have minimized the work of the Holy Spirit. We have lost touch with his personhood. The Holy Spirit is one person of the Trinity. We interact with the Holy Spirit as a person. He is our comforter, our friend, our intercessor. Paul teaches, "The Spirit helps us in our weakness. We do not know what we ought to pray for, but the Spirit himself intercedes for us through wordless groans" (Rom. 8:26). He knows what we want to say even when we don't have words for it. He ushers us into the presence of the Father and gives us wisdom, power, and love for others.

In fact, one mark of the Holy Spirit in a life is a supernatural ability to love. In the kingdom of God, this is the definition of power. Love covers sin, conquers death, and endures eternally. Paul writes, "God's love has been poured out into our hearts through the Holy Spirit, who has been given to us" (Rom. 5:5). Love is the headwaters, the place where the river starts. Spirit-led joy, peace, patience, kindness, goodness, faithfulness, gentleness, and self-control flow out of a loving center, and our ability to love is not self-generated or self-taught. It comes through the Holy Spirit.

The Holy Spirit Points Us to Jesus

The Holy Spirit is not only our connection with the Father; he reveals to us the truth about Jesus. Jesus taught, "When the Advocate comes, whom I will send you from the Father—the Spirit of truth who goes out from the Father—he will testify about me" (John 15:26). This is the primary work of the Holy Spirit in a life: it is to witness to the truth of Jesus Christ as Messiah and Savior. The Spirit always draws us back to Christ and shapes us to be more like him.

The great news is that the Holy Spirit makes Jesus real to us! What better gift could God give us? Not only does he save our lives from the pit of despair and hopelessness and redeem us from our slavery to sin, and not only does he fill us with love for God and neighbor, but he also makes a way for us to embrace the unfathomable truth of Jesus Christ! What in the natural world can only be a mystery to our limited minds, God has made accessible through the Holy Spirit.

The Holy Spirit Sanctifies Us

Methodist doctrine can be summed up in two words: *grace* and *holiness*. Some theologians believe that sanctification (or holiness) is the Wesleyan stream's great contribution to the Christian conversation. Our tradition isn't primarily about a form of worship, though we have written thousands of songs to God. It isn't primarily about getting people out of hell, though Wesley preached that we should flee the wrath to come. It doesn't claim to be Pentecostal, though we honor all the gifts of the Spirit. It isn't doctrinally rigid, though we certainly consider ourselves creedal. At its core, Methodism is about claiming a free gift of salvation then working it out daily with fear and trembling.

If the Holy Spirit is the match that sets our lives on fire, the means of grace are the kindling. Methodists believe spiritual practices such as prayer, Scripture study, community life, worship, acts of compassion, and the sacraments are motivators for moving us forward. For Wesley, the work of the Holy Spirit was welcomed and the means of grace took place in the context of community, where accountability is lodged. We examine our lives together and invite the Spirit to change our thinking about ourselves, the world around us, and our destiny. The lies of the enemy spoken over our lives are exposed and defeated. We grow in freedom as we are more and more conformed into his likeness. And as we become the person we were designed to be, we become more loving, more joyful, more at peace, more confident in calling on his power to transform others.

In short, Methodism is a call to live a holy life ignited by a Holy Spirit. A friend says that to live as a Christian without the indwelling of the Holy Spirit is like deep-sea diving without an oxygen tank. You can do it, but you'll never be able to dive as deeply as you want to. Your fear of suffocating will always force you back to the surface. But with the Holy Spirit, the holy life becomes abundant, joyful, peace-giving—a continual desire to grow deeper and deeper into the life of Christ.

The Holy Spirit Is Our Helper

Multiple times in John's gospel, the Holy Spirit is referred to by the Greek word *paraklétos*, which means "comforter, counselor, or one who walks with or helps another." The Spirit is given to us as a guide and friend to coach, correct, encourage, and empower. In his book *The Divided Flame*, theologian Howard A. Snyder explains that, "Wesley's understanding of the church and Christian experience can be described as charismatic because of the place of the Holy Spirit in his theology and because of his openness to the gifts of the Spirit."[2]

---

2. Howard Snyder, *The Divided Flame: Wesleyans and the Charismatic Renewal* (Eugene, OR: Wipf and Stock Publishers, 2011), 57.

The power to live abundantly and fruitfully is not in our effort but in the presence of the Holy Spirit. What separates the church of Jesus Christ from any other nonprofit is the power of God. Our tendency is to do without him until we get desperate. Yet, it is only in the power of God that we can move beyond our own efforts.

Luke reported, "When Jesus had called the Twelve together, he gave them power and authority to drive out all demons and to cure diseases, and he sent them out to proclaim the kingdom of God and to heal the sick" (Luke 9:1-2). For some of us, if we are honest, we dismiss these kinds of verses as merely for the Apostolic Era. But what if it is not? What if that is instructive for us today?

To cast out demons, cure diseases, proclaim the kingdom, or heal the sick can only happen in obedience to God and under the power of the Holy Spirit. If you have doubts, ask Methodists outside of North America. Other cultures often have a clearer picture of the spiritual forces at work in a situation and deeper reliance on supernatural solutions. The Holy Spirit is our helper, not in the sense that he takes up where we leave off, but in the sense that he fundamentally changes the character of our life and work.

This is the work of the Spirit as helper. We've said already that ultimately the Holy Spirit is given to send us into the world as witnesses, but the tools to do that are not ours to generate. The Holy Spirit endows us with gifts that open our lives more fully to participate in the work of the kingdom. We discover our spiritual gifts by watching how God is at work in us and through us so we can join him where he is at work in the world.

Paul gives us a start at understanding spiritual gifts in his letter to the Romans: "We have different gifts, according to the grace given to each one of us. If your gift is prophesying, then prophesy in accordance with your faith; if it is serving, then serve; if it is teaching, then teach; if it is to encourage, then give encouragement; if it is giving, then give generously; if it is it to lead, do it diligently, if it is to show mercy, do it cheerfully" (12:6-8).

In other words, watch for where God is working in your life, then follow the fruit. How have you been gifted for the sake of living like Jesus in this world?

The Holy Spirit Empowers Us

The gifts of the Spirit are made evident by the fruit they bear. The work of the Holy Spirit is to point us to Jesus and then to point us toward the world to welcome and advance the kingdom of God. Jesus said as much: "'As the Father has sent me, I am sending you.' And with that he breathed on them and said, 'Receive the Holy Spirit'" (John 20:21-22). The Holy Spirit sends us into the world to love as Jesus loved, and he gifts us with the resources we need in order to go. In his devotional classic *Ablaze for God*, missionary and revival leader Wesley Duewel writes, "We cannot light this fire. In ourselves we cannot produce it. No man can kindle in himself that celestial fire; it must come from the coal from the altar above."[3]

Brothers and sisters, a real Christian is never going to look like the rest of the world. Never. We are peculiar people. We are people who love profoundly, who hang on way past good sense, who believe the Holy Spirit uses odd people to advance the kingdom of God. Real Christians have the audacity to believe we are able to do the works that Jesus did and, in fact, greater works than that. We think serving other people is more fun than being served and that, in fact, God will show up when we do. We believe we are at our best when we are broken and poured out. We believe the God of the universe wants our partnership and that if we want to, we can welcome and advance the kingdom of God. We believe we are becoming more like Jesus every day, and that one day Jesus is coming home again—and will look for peculiar people who look like him.

---

3. Wesley Duewel, *Ablaze for God* (Grand Rapids, MI: Zondervan, 1989), 30.

What Next?

My own encounter with the Holy Spirit happened in my late twenties while I was on a spiritual retreat. Not long before, I made the statement to some church leaders that I'd never worshipped God in church. I was happy to be there, but I'd never really worshipped God. I went through all the motions, but it was not connected to my heart. I thought it was a problem with the church, not me, but then I went on this retreat, and God met me there in a way I didn't expect.

On this weekend, a group of people began to worship in song. It wasn't planned; it just happened. I wasn't used to that kind of spontaneous combustion—a sudden fire and the joyful presence of worship among regular people. In that setting, I suddenly felt the presence of the Holy Spirit in my life in a way I'd never felt before. For me, it was a physical feeling, although I don't think it always (or even usually) happens that way. For the first time in my life, though I'd been a believer for years, I felt a deep desire to worship God. That was the mark for me. It was this deep, passionate sense that God wanted me to worship him, to fall in love with him.

There was a great joy in my spirit. I am confident that in that moment, I experienced what some might call a baptism in the Holy Spirit. If you are wondering, I didn't speak in tongues (a biblical and supernatural gift often associated with the ministry of the Holy Spirit). Instead, I went home and applied to seminary. Many times since then, people who thought I should speak in tongues have prayed over me to receive the gift. I was always open to those prayers, because I figured if there is more God to be had, I want him. Nevertheless, it just didn't happen.

Years later in ministry, I was going through a serious spiritual battle. Those were really difficult days and I prayed a lot, sometimes for hours. One morning as I was praying, I felt something well up inside of me. It was as if (and I'm not going to be able to describe this perfectly) I could hear another language welling up in my being. Something was seeking to be spoken. I was in my own home alone so I let that voice rise up. It felt like a prayer, and—I'll be honest—it felt strange.

But just as I got uncomfortable, another thought came. It was to find a book that had been sitting on my shelf for a year. It was one of those books someone hands you on their way out of church on a Sunday morning. I'd not read it, just shelved it and forgot about it. At that prompting, I found the book and opened it to the first chapter. On the first page, first paragraph, the author recounted the story of the Navajo Marines who were embedded among U.S. Army troops during World War II. They were there to pass coded messages from the front lines back to the command post. They could pass messages from place to place without being intercepted because the Navajo language was unwritten and completely unknown to the enemy. And that, the author of this book said, is how God uses this spiritual language that the New Testament calls speaking in tongues. It is a code the enemy cannot break.

What a profound thought! I sensed God had given me a new weapon for fighting on the spiritual plane. And it came when I least expected it and most needed it. It was both hopeful and gentle. It was all gift, a renewed sense that there is no end to what God can do. I don't believe everyone who is filled with the Spirit will speak in tongues, but I absolutely believe everyone who is filled with the Spirit will receive gifts to empower them for life and ministry. There is *more*, brothers and sisters! Because there is no end to God, there is always more and we ought to want everything God has for us. If only we will trust him! He has so much more for us!

God is great and God is good! We ought to yearn for everything he has to offer. This is the heart of sanctification. This is what Paul preached and prayed over people he loved: "In all my prayers for all of you, I always pray with joy because of your partnership in the gospel from the first day until now, being confident of this, that he who began a good work in you will carry it on to completion until the day of Christ Jesus" (Phil. 1:4–6).

All over the world, God is pouring out the Holy Spirit. This is most apparent in Africa, Latin America, and parts of Asia, but even in the United States, God is changing lives, working wonders, and leading the church into ever-greater levels of faithfulness. The next Methodism will recover a deep understanding of God's sanctifying work. The maxim that "people never change" will be anathema on the lips of Methodists. People do change, we will affirm, because God changes them. As we seek the Holy Spirit in prayer, worship, the sacraments, and the reading of Scripture, we will do so with the expectation that the living God is really in our midst. Through healing, wisdom, tongues, sanctification, and other demonstrations of the power of the Spirit, God will make his power and will known to us.

The Holy Spirit wants to set our hearts on fire for the things that burn in the heart of God. Ask him to prepare the wood for you. Ask God to give you everything he has for you. Ask him to strike the match.

Questions for Discussion and Reflection

1. Many Methodists have not spent much time thinking about—much less experiencing—the person and work of the Holy Spirit. What has been your experience?

2. What are your biggest questions about the Holy Spirit?

3. "Methodism was launched as a Holy Spirit–infused global renewal movement." How does this statement sit with you as a United Methodist? Does it resonate? Sound unfamiliar? Seem overstated?

4. Read Acts 1:4–5. What did the Holy Spirit offer the disciples that they didn't already have?

5. Sanctification is "the Wesleyan stream's great contribution to the Christian conversation." In your own words, how would you define sanctification?

6. If the Holy Spirit's presence in our lives compels us to go into the world as witnesses, what does this say about your local church? How is your congregation participating in the work of welcoming and advancing the kingdom of God?

7. Everyone who is filled with the Holy Spirit will receive gifts to empower them for life and ministry. What gifts have you received?

8. In the future, Methodism must recover its expectation of the supernatural workings of the Holy Spirit. What is your hope for the power and presence of the Holy Spirit among Methodists?

Hiring a Sanctified Felon

Heather Hill

The congregation I serve has a reputation for being the kind of community that welcomes those who fall through the cracks of more traditional congregations. We often say we have the gift of hanging onto people long past good sense. Our people are solid, loving, welcoming, and gifted.

And some of them have lived hard lives.

But wow; they are givers. Once a month, we become a kind of mission outpost for our community. We offer prayer, job support, cancer support, medical screenings, and other things that might help families in crisis. We see between seventy-five and one hundred families on that one day every month, and we follow up to encourage them into community. We've also created a spiritual community with low- and no-income adults with disabilities in our downtown area. We worship and pray and study Scripture together, and we are often their ride to doctors' offices and grocery stores.

Every day we are challenged to hold Jesus together with these good things we're doing. Because if those we serve don't go some-place *spiritually*, what would make us any different from any other nonprofit? Isn't that the question Moses asked of the Lord in Exodus: "Is it not in your going with us that we are distinct from all the other people on earth?" (see 33:16)?

Surely we're supposed to be more than just good works. Surely the church of Jesus Christ is meant to be a demonstration of God's kingdom on earth.

About a year ago, we hired a director of adult discipleship, and that move was absolutely counterintuitive by the world's standards. Heather is her name. She's been with us for eight or nine years, but for most of those years, she played hokie-pokie with the church.

She put her foot in when she was clean but she'd disappear when she was using. Heather was a meth addict. At the end of it—of years of using—she was living in a cheap hotel, cooking and selling meth. Things were rough for her.

One night, she cried out to God. "Lord, I can't do this anymore. I need you to get me out of this . . . whatever it takes." God heard that prayer, and two days later, Jesus showed up in her hotel room. It was not a vision—Jesus was not decked out in a robe and sandals; instead, he was wearing a cop uniform, but there is no mistaking this was the hand of God.

Heather was arrested and got eighteen months in what we at Mosaic like to call in-depth Bible study (that's state prison). She went through a drug rehab program while she was in and God really got hold of her.

When she got out, she came home to Mosaic and was welcomed with open arms. She got into our recovery program and a small group. She went through our leadership incubator and began to lead a recovery group. She discovered a love for group life and a passion for leadership development She has distinguished herself among us as a spiritual leader. Every Sunday, our front row is full of her friends—addicts and former addicts inspired by her story.

So when it came time for us to hire a director of adult discipleship, there was one obvious choice. Which means that the person who coordinates our small-group life and inspires others to deeper discipleship is a felon—and we would not have it any other way.

Stories like Heather's are the *substance* of Wesleyan orthodoxy. We believe in the kind of religion talked about in James 1:27: "Religion that God our Father accepts as pure and faultless is this: to look after orphans and widows in their distress and to keep oneself from being polluted by the world." It is that passion for serving others without letting the world get the best of us. This is what makes Wesleyan theology so attractive. It is this insistence that its doctrines remain married to its practice. It is about doing ministry and doing it better and doing it in ways that highlight our brand of theology because that's what we have to offer the body of Christ.

Our congregation is comprised of Wesleyan, orthodox, Spirit-led, Jesus-loving, people-loving, mission-bent followers of Jesus who truly, passionately hunger for the whole world to be our parish. That's one of the reasons we hired a felon.

5

Loving God with an Undivided Heart

Maxie Dunnam

What distinguishes a Methodist? Ask John Wesley (1703-1791), the person who started it all, and a core point of his response would be, "Holiness of heart and life." This is at the center of what we need to recover.

Throughout Christian history, there have been those who rejected the beautiful fullness of orthodox faith. For example, the antinomians took liberties by rejecting what they considered to be legalism. Enthusiasts, on the other hand, gloried only in an emotional fanaticism. Still others embraced a form of Phariseeism that focused on the letter of the law to the exclusion of grace and mercy.

Wesley rejected these extremes. "If you preach doctrine only, the people will become antinomians; and if you preach experience only, they will become enthusiasts; and if you preach practice only, they will become Pharisees," he wrote. "But if you preach all these and do not enforce discipline, Methodism will become like a highly cultivated garden without a fence, exposed to the ravages of the wild boar of the forest."[1]

We are seeing the manifestations of this warning. Within the North American context of our Wesleyan movement we can see, too often, the trouble in our garden:

---

1. Fred Sanders, *Wesley on the Christian Life: The Heart Renewed in Love* (Wheaton, IL: Crossway, 2013), 41.

- experimentation with trendy pagan rituals and practices;
- consuming the world's goods without regard for others' poverty or working conditions;
- adopting the world's view of marriage and sexuality—abandoning our advocacy for celibacy in singleness and faithfulness in marriage between a man and a woman;
- resigning ourselves to the injustices of racial and gender prejudice;
- ignoring the historic church's long-standing protection of the unborn and the mother; and
- abandoning any sense of accountability among the bishops and leaders of our denomination.

The lingering threat of becoming nothing more than a dead sect is ever before us. We need a recovery of holiness of heart and life, the antidote of the relativism that is the operative dynamic of our culture. The Christian apologist Francis Schaeffer (1912–1984) once wrote, "If our reflex action is always accommodation, regardless of the centrality of the truth involved, there is something wrong. Just as what we may call holiness without love is not God's kind of holiness, so also what we call love without holiness is not God's kind of love."[2]

What happens when efforts to sustain systems of accountability, essential for the church to maintain its identity as the "holy Catholic Church," are ignored or even spurned for the sake of unity? While corporate unity is appealing, it is not our most important value. We need to discern between institutional unity and biblical unity. They are two different concepts. Before Jesus prayed that we would be one, he prayed that we would be set apart in the truth (see John 17:17).

---

2. Francis Schaeffer, The Great Evangelical Disaster (Wheaton, IL: Crossway, 1984), 64.

From God's point of view, truth is the basis for unity. Genuine Christian unity is forged in a common mission and a common conviction. The Bible knows nothing of unity simply for unity's sake, but vibrates with the unity that is forged in our mutual bondedness to new life in Christ, "the way and the truth and the life" (John 14:6).

Being Made Complete

Holiness is not a tangential option for Christians. At the same time, it must also become unbridled from the pejorative term "holier than thou." Holiness is not about casting judgment on others. Holiness, in the biblical sense, means living in sync with God's purpose and ways. So many of our painful trials and tribulations occur when we are living out of step with the holy rhythm of heaven. Holiness puts us back on track. The Trinity is our witness and provides a compelling exhortation. We read in the Old Testament that God said, "You shall be holy, for I the LORD your God am holy" (Lev. 19:2 NKJV). At first reading, that can appear like a heavy burden to carry, but as we grow in our relationship with God we discover that he is the one who enables and encourages us to walk the path with his guidance.

Jesus said something similar to the Old Testament passage in different words, "you shall be perfect, just as your Father in heaven is perfect" (Matt. 5:48 NKJV). Within a grace-filled faith, we make a clear distinction between the trap of "perfectionism" and the "being made whole" that Jesus meant. It is important to remember that the Greek word *telos* that is translated in English as "perfect" can also be understood as "mature, accomplished, or made complete."

The Holy Spirit, through inspiration given to Peter, confirms the call: "as He who called you *is* holy, you also be holy in all *your* conduct" (1 Pet. 1:15 NKJV). Throughout the Scriptures, there is the call for the people of God to be set apart as a holy people, living in sync with the will and way of God and moving forward with maturity to be made complete.

It is a common understanding among most scholars that holiness became Wesley's most distinctive doctrine. In 1733 he preached a sermon called "The Circumcision of the Heart," his most careful and complete statement of his understanding of "salvation from all sin, and loving God with an undivided heart." Noted Wesleyan scholar Dr. Albert Outler (1908–1989) stated that this sermon expounded "what would thenceforth become his most distinctive doctrine: Christian perfection understood as perfect love of God and neighbor, rooted in a radial faith in Christ's revelation of that love and its power."[3] This is the only sermon Wesley preached before his pivotal Aldersgate experience in 1738, where his heart was "strangely warmed," that he kept primarily in its original form, and used throughout his life in teaching Methodists.

Wesley's thoughts were rooted in Paul's call for a "circumcision" of the heart (see Romans 2:17–29). The Jews had allowed circumcision, the unique mark of their identification as a covenant people, to become superficial and meaningless. "Circumcision has value if you observe the law, but if you break the law, you have become as though you had not been circumcised" (Rom. 2:25). Paul follows this assessment of the situation by making his case clearly: "A person is not a Jew who is one only outwardly, nor is circumcision merely outward and physical. No, a person is a Jew who is one inwardly; and circumcision is circumcision of the heart, by the Spirit, not by the written code. Such a person's praise is not from other people, but from God" (Rom. 2:28–29).

Wesley never abandoned that sermon's ideal of holiness. However, prior to his Aldersgate experience, he consistently misplaced holiness. He was driven by the idea that one must be

---

3. John Wesley, *The Works of John Wesley*, vol. 1, ed. Albert C. Outler (Nashville, TN: Abingdon Press, 1984), 398–99.

holy in order to be justified or made right with God. This futile notion drove him to deep despondency, which eventually took him to Aldersgate. One of the most decisive shifts was a reversal of the order of salvation: justification preceded holiness, not vice versa.

Going On to Salvation

Wesley elegantly described holy love springing from an undivided heart in this fashion:

> It is the change wrought in the whole soul by the almighty Spirit of God when it is "created anew in Christ Jesus"; when it is "renewed after the image of God in righteousness and true holiness"; when the love of the world is changed into the love of God; pride into humility; passion into meekness; hatred, envy, malice, into a sincere, tender, disinterested love of all mankind.[4]

It all begins with repentance, when we are convinced and convicted of our sins, are genuinely sorry, and accept by faith what God has done for us in Jesus Christ. When we respond in faith to God's grace we are justified—made right with God—not because of our merit, but by divine grace. Justification is what God does *for* us, and sanctification (the second half of the whole gospel) is what God does *in* us. Love, not faith, becomes the final goal of the plan of salvation. The essence of sanctification is love in action, *loving God with an undivided heart*. By grace through faith we are not only justified, we are given newness of life, here and now, a transformation clearly reflecting a life that is no longer dominated by sin.

---

4. John Wesley, *Wesley's Fifty-Three Sermons*, ed. Edward H. Sugden (Nashville, TN: Abingdon, 1983), 511.

The Call of Scripture

The primary meaning of the word *sanctify* is "to set aside" or "to consecrate." In Hebrew, *qadas* means "to divide" or "to separate." When something is sanctified, it is set aside, removed from the profane, and consecrated to God, thus becoming holy. In the Old Testament, we read that the entire nation of Israel was sanctified to the Lord. God's admonition to Israel was: "I am the LORD your God; consecrate yourselves and be holy, because I am holy" (Lev. 11:44).

As a part of his farewell greeting to the Ephesian elders, Paul committed them to the Lord, naming them as they were, and underscoring what was promised: "Now I commit you to God and to the word of his grace, which can build you up and give you an inheritance among all those who are sanctified" (Acts 20:32).

Paul connected the two halves of salvation—justification and sanctification—in his word to the Corinthians. He had named some of the behaviors that divide people from the kingdom of God. Then he reminded them, "that is what some of you were," after which, he spoke that victorious word: "But you were washed, you were sanctified, you were justified in the name of the Lord Jesus Christ and by the Spirit of our God" (1 Cor. 6:11).

The call to holiness may sound like something new to most of the people in our United Methodist churches on any given Sunday. And yet it whispers, calls, and shouts throughout Scripture. Consider the biblical call to personal holiness in Romans 12:1-2:

Therefore, I urge you, brothers and sisters, in view of God's mercy, to offer your bodies as a living sacrifice, holy and pleasing to God—this is your true and proper worship. Do not conform to the pattern of this world, but be transformed by the renewing of your mind. Then you will be able to test and approve what God's will is—his good, pleasing and perfect will.

In his first letter to the Thessalonians, Paul expressed our sin and estrangement vividly:

It is God's will that you should be sanctified: that you should avoid sexual immorality; that each of you should learn to control your own body in a way that is holy and honorable, not in passionate lust like the pagans, who do not know God; and that in this matter no one should wrong or take advantage of a brother or sister (4:3-6).

The call is so pronounced that we Wesleyans believe that behind the biblical and theological themes of the meaning of creation, the fall of humanity, the understanding of law and grace, the meaning of justification, and the new birth, the ministry and work of the Holy Spirit is the call to holiness. Christian author and scholar C. S. Lewis (1898-1963) captured this sounding note that reverberates through the Bible with compelling clarity:

Christ says, "Give me All. I don't want so much of your time and so much of your money and so much of your work: I want You. I have not come to torment your natural self, but to kill it. No half-measures are any good. I don't want to cut off a branch here and a branch there, I want to have the whole tree down. I don't want to drill the tooth, or crown it, or stop it, but to have it out. Hand over the whole natural self, all the desires which you think innocent as well as the ones you think wicked—the whole outfit. I will give you a new self instead. In fact, I will you Myself: my own will shall become yours."[5]

The quest and expectation of everyone who is born of God is a life of holy love. As Lewis continued,

5. C. S. Lewis, *Mere Christianity* (New York: Simon & Schuster Touchstone, 1996), 171.

The Church exists for nothing else but to draw men into Christ, to make them little Christs. If they are not doing that, all the cathedrals, clergy, missions, sermons, even the Bible itself, are simply a waste of time. God became Man for no other purpose. It is even doubtful, you know, whether the whole universe was created for any other purpose.[6]

Expressing the love of God in a way that shapes our world, out of an undivided heart, is the goal of the Christian life.

Holiness of Heart and Life

The 1784 Christmas Conference in Baltimore, which formally established Methodism in America, made our mission clear. When the question was asked: "What can we rightly expect to be the task of Methodists in America?" The answer came clear and strong: "To reform the continent and spread scriptural holiness across the land."

What does all this mean? Simply put, yet profoundly challenging, it means that we Christians are to pursue holiness and that the church is to be that demonstration plot of holiness set down in an unholy world. Jesus said it means that we are to love God with all our heart, mind, soul, and strength, and our neighbor as ourselves (see Luke 10:27). To respond to sanctifying grace is to pay attention to all that is out of harmony with God's will and God's image within us, and through his grace be cleansed and delivered, believing that we can be cleansed and delivered. Every person who has been justified and born of the Spirit, from the moment of regeneration, has the promise of victory over sin and the devil. With the power of the Holy Spirit, we can pursue holiness and march forward in the fullness of faith.

---

6. Ibid.

This must not, however, be seen solely as personal. Wesley noted that the "gospel of Christ knows no religion but social; no holiness but social." He spoke of "inward holiness," love of God, and the assurance of God's love of us. Wesley also spoke of "outward holiness," love of neighbor, and deeds of kindness. He was fond of speaking of persons being "happy and holy." For him the experiences were not opposites, but actually one reality. As Wesley observed, "Christianity is essentially a social religion and to turn it into a solitary religion is to destroy it."[7]

Wesleyan scholars Drs. Kevin Watson and Andrew Thompson have both rightly reminded us not to equate social holiness with social justice. By social holiness, Wesley meant that Christians can't grow in holiness apart from community. That's the reason bands and class meetings and other accountability are so important; other people are essential for our growing in holiness.

However, we must be clear, holiness and becoming like Jesus necessarily compels us to confront social injustice. The late Dag Hammarskjöld (1905-1961), Swedish diplomat and former secretary-general of the United Nations, echoed this when he said, "The road to holiness necessarily passes through the world of action."[8]

The social impact of the Wesleyan revival and movement can hardly be exaggerated. The Wesleyan revival spawned innumerable reform movements—notably including the battle against slavery, as well as legislation addressing reform of working conditions. We should all carry within us the spirit of liberation that resonates off the page as Wesley wrote to William Wilberforce, blessing him and urging him on in his antislavery fight in England. "Go on," he said, "in the name of God and in the power of his might, till even

---

7. Paul Wesley Chilcote, *Recapturing the Wesley's Vision* (Downers Grove, IL: InterVarsity Press, 2004), 49.
8. Dag Hammarskjöld, *Markings* (New York: Knopf, 1964), 122.

American slavery (the vilest that ever saw the sun) shall vanish away before it."[9]

From its beginning, the Methodist movement has addressed poverty, slavery, prison conditions, substance abuse, war—and in more recent times, sex trafficking, gender equality, public education, racial equality, and women's rights. We know from the Old Testament prophet that God has a fearsome judgment of a people who "sell . . . the needy for a pair of sandals" (Amos 2:6). And know from Jesus himself that our judgment will be based on how we respond to "the least of these" (Matt. 25:40).

If Wesleyans wish to reflect the character of Christ, pursuing holiness with an undivided heart and loving our neighbors sacrificially, how then should we act on a local and global level when we consider the following:

- economic and social structures that keep the poor bereft of the same educational and cultural advantages as the balance of the population;
- a currently renewed nuclear arms race that clouds the world with ominous fear and drains the financial resources of nations;
- a retributive prison system that contributes more to making a criminal society than preventing crime and reforming offenders;
- a society that redefines human sexuality and gender identity and that trivializes casual divorce and the value of nuclear families; and
- an immigration policy that forgets the biblical call to "welcome the stranger" and show hospitality to the homeless?

---

9. Maxie Dunnam, *The Christian Way: A Wesleyan View of Our Spiritual Journey* (Grand Rapids, MI: Zondervan, 1987), 91.

How Then Must We Live?

First, exercise faith. The One who saves is the One who sanctifies. God does not require what is not possible by grace through faith. "Such a faith as this cannot fail to show evidently the power of him that inspires it, by delivering his children from the yoke of sin, and 'purging their consciences from dead works,'" wrote Wesley, "by strengthening them so that they are no longer constrained to obey sin in the desire thereof; but instead of 'yielding their members unto' it, 'as instruments of unrighteousness' they now 'yield' themselves entirely 'unto God as those that are alive from the dead.'"[10]

Second, don't give up pursuing freedom from sin. Inherent in God's call to holiness and maturity is the promise of fulfillment. God makes gracious provision for all he asks of us. Climatically, after the glorification of Christ, the sanctifying grace of the Holy Spirit was accorded in full measure to believers. So by the power of the Holy Spirit, sanctifying grace gives us power over sin. Paul admonishes us, "Count yourselves dead to sin and alive to God in Christ Jesus" (Rom. 6:11). No longer are we to be "slaves to sin" (Rom. 6:6). Settle this truth solidly in your mind, and call often to awareness: God's grace is more powerful than the lure of temptation.

Third, be willing to be equipped for ministry. By the power of the Holy Spirit, sanctifying grace equips us for ministry. One of the biblical meanings of sanctification is to be "consecrated for the services of God." Being equipped for ministry has special relevance to the notion of holiness. The way someone introduced Mother Teresa makes the case: "She gave her life first to Christ, and then through Christ to her neighbor. That was the end of her biography and the beginning of her life."

Holiness is a call not just to individuals but for the community of faith to act as the body of Christ in the world. As the body

---

10. See Romans 6:12–13; *The Works of John Wesley*, 406.

of Christ, the church is to be his presence in the world, seeing with the eyes, speaking with the voice, healing with the hands of Christ among the poor and the elderly, among those who are economically deprived and politically oppressed, among the strangers in our midst, among the emotionally and mentally ravaged, among those in the tenacious grip of alcohol and drugs, among our ethnically divided communities, among the homeless and the single moms living on the edge of despair, and among prisoners and ex-convicts who see little hope of acceptance and jobs.

In all of this and the unrecognized suffering around us, we must also breathe with Christ's Spirit. As his body, we are not only a human organization, we are a spiritual organism. Our life is the life of Christ, empowered by the Holy Spirit. The Spirit continues to blow through the church, which is Christ's body. And as the Spirit blows, the gates of hell cannot prevail against the church.

Last, embrace experiences that will require you to grow. By the power of the Holy Spirit, sanctifying grace provides us an experience in which we can grow. We are completely cleansed from sins committed. Though our sin nature may not be completely eradicated, we can be so perfected in our bent toward love that our sin nature is sorely diminished in power and no longer dominates our will. Our spiritual disciplines will enable us to be moment-by-moment dependent upon God under the lordship of the indwelling Christ.

Questions for Discussion and Reflection

1. Holiness is a loaded term! For many of us, it conjures up terms like *perfectionism, legalism,* or *judgmentalism*. Setting the "isms" aside, what does holiness mean to you?

2. How does your idea of holiness change if you think of it as being complete, mature, or whole, rather than perfect?

3. What does loving God with an undivided heart look like for you this week?

4. In our session on the Holy Spirit, we began talking about sanctification as a Wesleyan distinctive. In this session, we take that conversation further. What new idea or thought do you have about sanctification after this teaching?

5. C. S. Lewis said all faith activity is a waste of time if we ignore the point that Jesus' coming was to make us like Christ. Do you agree or disagree?

6. "Holiness and becoming like Jesus necessarily compels us to confront social injustice." What is the connection between personal holiness and serving or influencing the world around us?

7. Why do you think sanctification can only happen in the context of community?

8. How can Methodism benefit from a renewed interest in the doctrine of sanctification in the future?

WITNESS

Our God of Deliverance

Kenneth Levingston

In Daniel 3, King Nebuchadnezzar sets up a ninety-foot god, nine feet wide, and says, "Every time you hear the music, every time you hear the praise, I want you to bow down to this god because it's just saying that you're a part of the team, that you're part of the culture in which you find yourself." In his audience are three boys: Shadrach, Meshach, and Abednego. They wear the clothes of the culture, and work in the jobs offered by the culture, but they won't bow down to another god. It was as if they were saying, "I can work with you, I can barbeque with you, but I can't bow down with you. I can't bow down unless we're talking about the true and living God."

Shadrach, Meshach, and Abednego say to Nebuchadnezzar, "King, may you live forever! Bless you and your mama and all your kinfolk, but I can't bow down because there is no other God but the living God of Israel." The king replies, "How dare you stand up and tell me there's another god? How dare you stand up and tell me there's an absolute truth other than *my* truth? I'll throw you in the fire." They say, "King, we don't know what our God *will* do, but we know what he *can* do. You can put us in the fire but our God can keep us."

And today, in our current climate, we must say the same: "You can put us in the fire, but our God can keep us."

Most people think this is a story about the faith of Hebrew boys, but this is really a story about the faithfulness of God. In this heated time, we need to be reminded that the God we serve is able to keep us. He is greater than our fear, greater than our anxiety. God will get in the fire with us, and God will deliver us from a world of false gods. And we do live in a world with many false gods. Consider these:

- *Salvation without sacrifice.* Let me tell you, God takes my sin seriously. He died for my sin. He died because I'm a sinner and could not save myself. My response to that salvation must be a willingness to enter into sanctification—to sacrifice my old life for the One who saved me.

- *Sanctification without submission.* We want to be filled with the Holy Ghost without submission to the Word of God, the will of God, or the clear teaching of Scripture. We want justification without sanctification. But this is not the spirit of the very movement to which we've committed. At the heart of Methodism is the joy and freedom found in working out our salvation daily.

- *Mercy and grace without truth and transformation.* Mercy without truth? Grace without transformation? Mercy and grace without justice is an illusion. It is temporary, at best; more often, it is an idol. I love mercy, but mercy didn't save me. The blood of Jesus saved me, and mercy is the agent he used.

- *Forgiveness without faithfulness.* "I'm alright, you're alright, everybody's okay." This feels great, but it has no lasting power. True kindness leads to repentance, nothing less.

I pray that God will raise up some more Shadrachs, Meshachs, and Abednegos. I believe he will also raise up some Sheniquas, some Michelles, and some Elisias. I believe he is raising some men and women who will stand up and say, "God, I draw the line here. Your Word is real, your Word is alive. You are my God. I will not bow down, I will not give up, I will not give in. You are an awesome God. I want my name to be on the list of the faithful. I want to join Abel, Enoch, and Noah. I want to join Abraham, Moses, Joseph, and Hannah. God, I want my name on the list."

God is raising up a new generation of faithful followers. The same God who spoke in Exodus 20 is speaking today. I'm talking about a God who will make things happen if we're willing to submit ourselves and say, "There is no other God; I will not bow down."

6

The Dynamism of Discipleship

Andrew Forrest

One of the most remarkable growth trajectories in Christian history occurred among the Methodists in the United States from 1776 to 1850. In that nearly seventy-five-year span of time between the American Revolution and the Civil War, the Methodist Church grew from 8,500 members to about 1.2 million—an astounding growth rate of 14,000 percent.

From a present-day perspective, the news is not so positive. Since it was reconstituted as the United Methodist Church in 1968, American Methodism has *been steadily losing members every year*—losing more than four million members in the last fifty years.

Why? What accounts for both the remarkable growth of Methodism in the early days of the United States, and its recent and regrettable decline? The answer to that question involves two simple words: *make disciples*.

Those same two words provide the answer to a related question about the growth of the early church itself. As sociologist and world religions scholar Rodney Stark puts it in his book, *The Triumph of Christianity*:

> [Jesus] was a teacher and miracle worker who spent nearly all of his brief ministry in the tiny and obscure province of Galilee, often preaching to outdoor gatherings. A few listeners took up his invitation to follow him, and a dozen or so became his devoted disciples, but when he was

executed by the Romans his followers probably numbered no more than several hundred. *How was it possible for this obscure Jewish sect to become the largest religion in the world?*[1]

The challenge to "make disciples" was the catalyst that caused that obscure Jewish sect to grow into the largest religion in the world. It does more than just provide an explanation for what happened; it also offers us a way forward today. These two words are spiritual dynamite, full of power to transform the world. These two words are a promise and a hope to anyone who takes them seriously.

The Mission of the Church

Why does the church exist? What is its purpose? An uninformed observer, after attending United Methodist churches throughout the country, might conclude that the church exists to host worship services on Sundays; feed the poor in soup kitchens; or mobilize marchers for a political cause.

And that observer would be wrong. Although churches should host services on Sundays and be in ministry to the poor and work for change in society, none of these worthy activities are the actual mission of the church.

Instead, the mission of the church is to make disciples. This mission is the reason that early Methodism flourished, that recent Methodism has languished, and that an obscure Jewish sect has become the largest religion in the world.

This mission is found in its original context in the Great Commission of Jesus: "Therefore go and make disciples of all nations, baptizing them in the name of the Father and of the Son

---

1. Rodney Stark, *The Triumph of Christianity: How the Jesus Movement Became the World's Largest Religion* (New York: HarperCollins, 2011), 1, emphasis added.

and of the Holy Spirit, and teaching them to obey everything that I have commanded you" (Matt. 28:19-20).

A disciple is a student. A Christian disciple is someone who is in apprenticeship to Jesus, so as to learn the Jesus way of living. According to Jesus, this is the point of the church: the church exists to make disciples.

Go Everywhere and Teach Everything

The mission of the church is to go wherever people are and teach them everything Jesus said and did. Jesus does not tell his followers that their mission is to have vibrant worship services or to feed the poor or to be engaged politically; he tells them to make disciples. If we take Jesus' command seriously, we will inevitably host weekly worship services and be in ministry with the poor and we'll be engaged politically, *but these things are the results and implications of the church's mission (i.e., discipleship) and not the primary mission itself.*

Discipleship to Jesus is emphatically not narrowly confined to what we might call habits of personal piety such as prayers, moral living, and Sunday school attendance. Discipleship is not something we do for a few minutes in the morning before we engage with the real world. Note the words of Jesus in the Great Commission: "teach them to obey *everything* that I have commanded you" (emphasis mine). Even the most cursory reading of the Gospels shows that Jesus was not merely concerned with matters of personal piety.

Likewise, discipleship to Jesus must be much more than habits of personal piety in our own lives. Discipleship affects all of life, from the personal to the political. After all, from a human perspective, it wasn't personal piety that got Jesus killed—he was killed because he was a threat to the powers and principalities. Jesus was not killed because he was irrelevant to real life, but because he was specifically concerned with real life.

Put On Your Oxygen Mask First

As a pastor, I've seen the following many times: a husband and a wife have children who become the focus and emotional fulfillment of their lives. They would do anything for their children's happiness, and they often do. Over time, this focus on the children causes the husband and wife to neglect their own relationship, and the marriage begins to wither. One day, the husband and the wife come to the conclusion that divorce is inevitable, and they break the news to the children. Unintentionally, the parents' apparent focus on the children—at the expense of the marriage—ends up harming the children in the long run.

First things must come first; our problem is that we tend to focus on second things, and wonder why we aren't getting first results. There is a reason the flight attendant tells you to put your oxygen mask on first, before tending to your child. After all, if you asphyxiate and keel over, there will be no one to help your son or daughter. First things must come first.

The situation in many of our churches today is that we are spending our time focusing on good things, but they are secondary concerns rather than our first mission. Let me reemphasize, the problem is not that worship services and food banks and political engagement are bad things. In fact, they are good and necessary things we need to be doing, and things that Jesus commanded. The problem is that putting these *outcomes* of discipleship in place of discipleship itself means that we are setting ourselves up to fail, like a panicked mother who forgets to put on her own oxygen mask.

For example, hosting a vibrant worship service is not our first mission, though it is a good thing—a very good thing. If we are actively and effectively making disciples, we will have vibrant worship services on Sunday morning. But, if we come to believe that vibrant worship services themselves are the point and put our efforts toward that end, at best we'll have superficial shows that lack the power to change hearts, and at worst our churches will be empty.

In a different vein, some modern United Methodist churches have mistakenly concluded that you can have social justice without discipleship. It didn't work for the Marxists, and it won't work for the Methodists. This is because social justice is an abstract idea that is impossible without real men and women bringing it about. For example, if we want to see racial justice in America, it won't happen apart from training men and women to die to themselves and sacrifice on behalf of their neighbors. In other words, it won't happen without discipleship. To put discipleship first is not to abandon social justice. On the contrary, the only way to move toward social justice is through the ancient practices of discipleship.

There is a reason the world is such an unjust place, and that reason is sin. It makes people selfish and it makes people cruel. The only cure for sin is the gospel, and it is through the journey of discipleship that Jesus "breaks the power of cancelled sin," as Charles Wesley proclaimed. If the church focuses on training people to be apprentices to Jesus, that effort will unleash ferocious forces of compassion into the world. We'll do *more* work with the poor, not less.

Branches Don't Need Management Consultants

At the Last Supper, Jesus spoke to his disciples about vines, branches, commitment, connectedness, and fruitfulness. Here are a few selected verses: "I am the true vine, and my Father is the vine-grower. . . . Just as the branch cannot bear fruit by itself unless it abides in the vine, neither can you unless you abide in me. I am the vine, you are the branches. . . . If you abide in me, and my words abide in you, ask for whatever you wish, and it will be done for you.

My Father is glorified by this, that you bear much fruit and become my disciples" (John 15:1-8 NRSV).

The branches don't strain and they don't strategize; the branches produce fruit naturally, effortlessly, because they are connected to the vine. Jesus promised his disciples that if they stayed connected to him, then their ministry would be fruitful. To see an example of fruitful ministry, we look to the ministry of Jesus himself and we see that through him, "the blind receive their sight, the lame walk, the lepers are cleansed, the deaf hear, the dead are raised, and the poor have good news brought to them" (Matt. 11:5 NRSV). Once again, a focus on disciple-making is not a focus on personal piety: the mission of disciple-making is the only way to actually transform the world.

It Worked!

"How was it possible for this obscure Jewish sect to become the largest religion in the world?"

When we revisit Rodney Stark's excellent question, the answer seems clearer. Christianity grew because the followers of Jesus did *exactly* what he told them to do: they made disciples by going everywhere and teaching everything Jesus commanded.

Churches grow when they make disciples. It's possible to grow churches through the superficial, but it won't last—in that case both the people in the church and the church itself will be like the seed that fell on rocky soil. To experience true and lasting growth, we need to focus on making disciples.

One of the criticisms of disciple-making is the charge that the real work of the church will be neglected. What that is meant to convey is that if we focus on making disciples we will become inward-focused, irrelevant, and neglectful of those in need.

What's fascinating, however, is the original disciples trained other disciples, who trained others, and that, in the early days of the church, these fledgling apprentices to Jesus were known *even by their enemies* for their care for others—particularly the poor. For example, during the plagues that afflicted the Roman Empire, Christians stayed behind in the infected cities to care for the sick, though this action meant that they often died themselves. As Professor Stark explains:

> Indeed, the impact of Christian mercy was so evident that in the fourth century when the emperor Julian attempted to restore paganism, he exhorted the pagan priesthood to compete with the Christian charities. In a letter to the high priest of Galatia, Julian urged the distribution of grain and wine to the poor, noting that "the impious Galileans [Christians], in addition to their own, support ours, [and] it is shameful that our poor should be wanting our aid."[2]

A disciple learns from his teacher. The early Christians learned from Jesus to lay down their lives and love their neighbors as themselves. The church's focus on discipleship meant that the church grew, because the pagans saw the witness of the disciples of Jesus and were convinced of the truth of the gospel.

The gospel *is* true and actions based on that truth *will* be effective. If you rotate crops and fertilize correctly, you will have a bountiful harvest. If you base your life on the words of Jesus, the things he said would happen, will happen. The words of Jesus aren't a theory: *they are the truth about the world itself.* The words of Jesus are as true as gravity, and as inescapable.

For two thousand years, whenever the church has taken the Great Commission seriously and put its effort into making disciples, it has flourished. This is the story of the church, and it is the story of the early days of the Methodist movement.

---

2. Ibid., 118.

It Worked in Methodist History

Churches abound in the United States, but places that take discipleship seriously are rare. In our larger society, there is a growing gap between the rich and the poor, and that gap shows up in churches too. Church has become a place for the middle and upper classes, with fewer and fewer poor people attending church regularly, if at all. All the while, the institutional church has become bureaucratic, thwarts innovation, and seems to exist purely for its own preservation.

This was also the situation in England in the middle of the eighteenth century. In other words, John Wesley's ministry took place in a culture and a church that in some ways is very similar to our own. He was convinced that being a Christian ought to mean that you were becoming more and more like Jesus. For Wesley, the gospel was not merely about forgiveness of sins, but about God's power and desire to make the believer holy.

This Wesleyan understanding of the gospel is evident in a line from Charles Wesley's well-known hymn quoted earlier: "He breaks the power of cancelled sin." God forgives, and then he frees. Apprentices in the Jesus way become the kind of people who become more and more filled with love and less and less enslaved to sin. Of course, this was not a new idea in the church (it's an idea that leaps off the pages of the New Testament itself), but it was an idea that needed to be reheard in eighteenth-century England. Wesley turned his considerable organizational skills to the task of making disciples, and the result was wild success.

The Methodist Method: Classes and Bands

When Wesley's enemies first labeled him a "Methodist" in the 1720s, they meant the term to be derisive. But, Wesley adopted it as his own, and the name certainly captured his approach to discipleship: it was methodical. His ministry had a clear goal—to make disciples—and a clear strategy to do it.

Wesley preached up and down Britain, and wherever he went, he organized the Methodists into small groups that he called "classes." The point of the class was to have the members "watch over one another in love," and the main tool the class leader used was a question that was asked of each member: "How is it with your soul?"[3]

Classes were co-ed groups of about twelve people, with a class leader who was the spiritual shepherd of the others. In America throughout the first century of Methodism, you couldn't be a Methodist unless you were in a class meeting. In other words, the entire purpose of the Methodist movement was discipleship, to train people to become more like Jesus. The Methodists took discipleship so seriously that if you weren't willing to do the same, you couldn't be a Methodist.

These kinds of small group interactions can have transforma-tive power in our contemporary age. John is a young father and attorney in my congregation who was living life the way the culture told him to live it: in excess. His goal was more hours, more money, more stuff. Unsurprisingly, this way of life wasn't bringing him joy or peace, and he and his family started attending our church. John began attending one of our small groups (our version of the class meeting) and his life radically changed: he began reading Scripture and digging into theology; he began to see his work as a lawyer as a means to an end and not as an end in itself; he felt called to work toward reconciliation in his family; he got engaged in a high-profile legal aid movement. In other words, he began to intentionally

---

3. Kevin Watson has an excellent book, *The Class Meeting*, that contains prac-tical steps pastors can take to implement the Wesleyan class meeting today. It is my experience that the changes and supplements to historic Methodist practices I outline can be used by the Holy Spirit to help people become more like Jesus. And people who are more like Jesus are people who transform the world. See Kevin Watson's *The Class Meeting: Reclaiming a Forgotten (and Essential) Small Group Experience* (Wilmore, KY: Seedbed Publishing, 2014).

apprentice himself to Jesus, and things started happening as a result.

As an additional model of discipleship training, Wesley organized Methodists into small, single-sex accountability groups called "bands." (He used the word not in the musical Rolling Stones sense, but in the older English sense along the lines of "Robin Hood and his band of merry men.") In the bands, you shared your sins from the previous week and after you had confessed them, another member of the band reminded you of the good news of 1 John: "If we confess our sins, he who is faithful and just will forgive us our sins and cleanse us from all unrighteousness" (1:9 NRSV).

Once again, this kind of discipleship group can translate into our contemporary setting. Mary is a young single woman in our congregation who was invited to church by a friend. Mary grew up with an absent father, and with the anger and hurt that a father's absence produces in a child. Through the unglamorous habit of meeting regularly with the women in her small group (we have a few single-sex groups similar to the bands), Mary began to experience the love of her heavenly Father. That relationship has begun to heal her, from the inside out. All she did was show up, and the Lord did the rest.

Historically, discipleship made Methodism extremely fruitful. When they arrived in America, the Methodists made the class meeting central to their ministry plan and, as I noted earlier, the Methodist church in America experienced astounding growth during the first seventy-five years of the United States.

"I Do Not Think It Means What You Think It Means"

The key to Wesley's discipleship method was his insight that "there is no holiness without social holiness." This pithy statement requires clarification. Today, many people mistakenly assume that

Wesley meant "social justice" where he said "social holiness." While Wesley was absolutely committed to social justice, what Wesley meant was that it is not possible to become more like Jesus on your own—you need a group of people around you.[4]

Wesley's emphasis on social holiness shouldn't surprise us, because we know that the best way to train for a marathon, lose weight, quit drinking, or learn Spanish is to do it alongside a group of like-minded people who are committed to the same goal and are willing to hold us accountable. Wesley realized this was also true with regard to discipleship, which is why he said that there is no holiness without social holiness: if you want to be like Jesus, you'll need to do it along with others.

Unfortunately, by 1850, the Methodists in America began to relax their focus on discipleship: class meetings moved from required to optional to nonexistent, and the church placed its energies in other places such as in Sunday school and education. Education is important, but it is not our primary mission. It is not surprising that when we abandoned our primary mission, we began to decline in numbers and influence. The sad trend away from intentional discipleship has continued to the present-day, and so has Methodist decline.

The United Methodist Church in America is at a crossroads, and most of the messages on the signposts aren't encouraging. I do not believe, however, that God is finished with us. We have the history and the opportunity to reclaim a Wesleyan emphasis on discipleship. Our method that was so wildly successful in the eighteenth and nineteenth centuries can be effective today, but it will require tweaking.

---

4. Taken within its 1739 context, Wesley's point was drawn from the truth that the gospel of Christ was not a solitary religion. "'Holy solitaries' is a phrase no more consistent with the gospel than holy adulterers. The gospel of Christ knows of no religion but social; no holiness but social holiness" (the preface to his 1739 edition of *Hymns and Sacred Poems*).

How to Make Disciples in Twenty-First-Century America

Each of the imperatives of discipleship listed below will be insufficient on its own, but taken together they are a way forward for the Methodist movement and will lead to fruitfulness.

Teach Scripture

During my ordination interviews, one of the men across the table told me that I "quote Scripture like a Baptist." I understood that he meant the remark as a compliment, but it was also deeply revealing. His implication was that Methodists don't know Scripture. He was right, of course; our people are biblically illiterate.

In previous generations, people would learn the basic stories of Scripture from school and from the culture, but today the only place people can go to learn Scripture is to church, and our churches are doing a poor job of teaching the Bible. The early Methodist pastors could have assumed that even the least-churched in their communities had a working knowledge of Scripture's stories, but this is no longer the case.

If we are going to take discipleship seriously, we are going to have to teach Scripture. There is no discipleship without the teaching of Scripture. Pastors need to recover their identities as Bible teachers. Scripture was central to Jesus, and if we are his apprentices, it will be to us. In my own experience, I have never seen an example of spiritual growth in someone that happened apart from that person's study of Scripture. You cannot be a disciple of Jesus without immersing yourself in Scripture.

Our people need basic catechetical instruction in the Scripture. We need to teach the grand sweep of Scripture, as well as the sort of basic information that school children learned in the eighteenth century: the names and places of the books of the Bible, their general themes, etc. It is almost not possible to teach Scripture at too basic a level.

Teach Prayer

Prayer has always been difficult, but our culture has made it more difficult. We are constantly distracted and harried, reaching into our pockets for our phones, unable to be still and know God. Jesus was well-known for his tendency to withdraw to lonely places to pray.

Wesley was well-known for his discipline in prayer, and we modern Methodists will need to imitate his example. We will need to teach our people to pray in the language of the Scriptures. We will need to teach people to pray in public. We will need to teach them to pray the desires of their hearts. And we will need to practically teach them *how* to create the space for prayer. Jesus withdrew to solitary places to pray, but where are our solitary places?

Jesus wants us to be fruitful, and prayer is like water for spiritual fruit; without it, we'll never be able to produce the outcomes he has for us. Disciples of Jesus are people who are desperate to learn to pray as Jesus prayed.

Connect People Together

Scripture and prayer are necessary but not sufficient. We will fail at making disciples unless we also connect like-minded people together who can watch over one another in love as they seek to imitate Christ. Relational discipleship was the engine of the Methodist method, and we need its power today. Here, however, we find another significant cultural hurdle.

The only qualification you had to have in early Methodism to join a class meeting was a "desire to flee from the wrath the come." But we live in a culture that teaches that God is like a cosmic Santa

Claus: he just wants us to be happy, and if we happen to be naughty instead of nice—and none of us is perfect, right?—he'll just pat us on the head and give us good stuff anyway. In early Methodism, in contrast, people were actually *afraid* of divine judgment. That is no longer the case.

In my experience, many of the people who come to our churches will not initially bring with them the deep desire for holiness required to make class meetings work. Class meetings only work if people actually want to grow in faith. If people aren't committed to show up regularly and take the "How is your life in God?" question seriously, our class meetings will not be effective—they can't be forced.[5]

But over time, as people spend time in Scripture and prayer, God will shape their desires so that they will actually *want* to take their discipleship seriously. And, over time, as people watch over one another in love through modern versions of the class and band meetings, they will have increased hunger for prayer and Scripture. Each component builds on the others. And when that happens, that's when our churches catch fire.

What If?

What if people are hungry for discipleship and they don't even know it? Discipleship is not something that is tacked on to real life. Rather, discipleship is the essence of real life itself. A disciple is someone who will learn from Jesus how to live with joy and peace in all situations. A disciple is someone who will grow in love so that he or she will sacrifice for the good of others.

People are hungry for discipleship because discipleship is God's plan for our lives, and God has asked us to tell them. And for two

---

5. The language used in the eighteenth- and nineteenth-century class meetings, "How is it with your soul?" is antiquated, and a better question in today's vernacular might be, "How is your life in God?"

thousand years, wherever the church has taken discipleship seriously, the world *has* been transformed.

What if, in our lifetimes, God saw fit to use the Methodists in the same great way he used us two hundred years ago? What if we saw a great explosion of faith and maturity in the Western world? What if we are right on the edge of the Third Great Awakening?

That's what I'm believing for. What about you?

Questions for Discussion and Reflection

1. Why does the church exist? What is its purpose?
2. If your church was destroyed by a tornado, would your community lose anything or would your church members only lose a building in which to meet weekly?
3. How does your church activity calendar and your annual budget reflect your commitment to form Jesus' apprentices?
4. How does your daily routine show that you're a Jesus apprentice?
5. Read John 15:1–8. What does this passage tell a follower of Jesus about a life connected to Christ and what that looks like?
6. Wesley said, "There is no holiness without social holiness." What is the difference between social holiness and social justice? What is the value of social holiness as Wesley defined it?
7. Describe your experience with small-group discipleship.
8. How is it with your soul?

WITNESS

Jesus on the Margins

Jorge Acevedo

As followers of Jesus in the Wesleyan way, we do not choose between the great commandments. We are compelled to both love God with all our hearts, souls, minds, and strength, *and* love our neighbor as ourselves (see Matthew 22:37–39). We believe in faith and action. Both. As followers of Jesus, faith is lived best when we work on our prayer lives and work to end human trafficking. Our local churches are being faithful to the way of Jesus when our hands are lifted high in transcending worship and our hands are reaching low to work with the poor.

This was part of the genius of the Wesleys and the early Methodists. Early Methodists searched for innovative places and ways to find ports of entry where the Holy Spirit went before them to share the good news of Jesus. Some of the early Methodist ports of entry included field preaching, literacy efforts, medical care for the sick, homes for orphans and widows, care for people with physical disabilities, opposition to slavery, inexpensive mass publications, and economic development projects for the poor.

"By salvation I mean, not barely, according to the vulgar notion, deliverance from hell, or going to heaven," wrote Wesley, "but a present deliverance from sin, a restoration of the soul to its primitive health, its original purity; a recovery of the divine nature; the renewal of our souls after the image of God, in righteousness and true holiness, in justice, mercy and truth."[6]

---

6. *The Works of The Reverend John Wesley, A.M.* (New York: J. Emory and B. Waugh, 1831), vol. 5, 35.

One of the early Methodist bases for works of piety and works mercy was the Foundery in London. The main room of the building was large enough to seat fifteen hundred people. At one time, the Foundery had been a place for casting cannons. After a serious explosion in 1716, the weapons operation moved to Woolwich. The Foundery remained damaged and unused until 1738, when John Wesley either rented or purchased it and organized the Methodist Society there.

In addition to worship services, other ministries occurred on the premises such as a school for marginalized children and the dispensing of money from a loan fund for poor people to help prevent them from paying exorbitant interest to others (think microloans). This is what early Methodists did.

Several years ago, God opened a door for Grace Church, the congregation I serve, to minister with persons with disabilities and their families—a marginalized and unreached people group in our community. We discovered that the divorce rate among families with children with disabilities is significantly higher than the national average. Mothers with children with disabilities typically die earlier. We also learned that there are limited community resources in Florida after a person with disabilities turns twenty-two years old.

In response, we first began a Sunday morning "buddy" program that integrated younger children with disabilities into our children's ministry. Then we began a monthly three-hour respite program for families with children with disabilities. But the most exciting ministry we began was a ministry called Exceptional Entrepreneurs (EE). This ministry had a vision to create employment and training opportunities for young adults. And it has exploded.

This ministry is a safe place where persons with disabilities learn to make products that are sold. Several of the students receive a paycheck. Bible studies are a regular part of this fresh expression of church. About two years ago one of the volunteers was led to Christ and baptized on a Sunday morning. Several of our EE students began to ask questions about being baptized themselves. One evening I met with the students and their families to talk about being baptized and following Jesus, and later that month, we baptized four of them.

As I drove home that morning after their baptisms, I told the Lord, "Take me because it can't get any better than this!"

This passion to be in ministry with the poor, addicted, and marginalized is who we are as Methodists. This is our spiritual DNA; it's in our blood. This is who we are and what we do as the people called Methodists.

7

The Church's Global DNA

Kimberly Reisman

After this I looked, and there before me was a great multitude that no one could count, from every nation, tribe, people and language, standing before the throne and before the Lamb. They were wearing white robes and were holding palm branches in their hands. And they cried out in a loud voice: "Salvation belongs to our God, who sits on the throne, and to the Lamb."

—Revelation 7:9-10

This is the vision God gave to John of Patmos. It celebrates a multilingual, multiethnic, and multinational family. All colors, all languages, all DNAs. This is the church—the church that God sees. This will be the church of the everlasting future. This is the direction we are headed.

In my work with World Methodist Evangelism, I have learned that no matter where I travel around the globe, it seldom lines up with my assumptions. It always ends up being different than I had expected. For example, when I traveled to Vladivostok, Russia, I expected to meet Russians who looked like, say, Dolph Lundgren or Boris Yeltsin. Instead, I encountered people who looked dramatically different than my preconceived notion: Korean-Russians, Russians from Central Asia, Chinese-Russians, and others.

My experience in Central Asia was similar. Arriving in Kyrgyzstan, bordered by China, Afghanistan, and Uzbekistan, I anticipated a more "Asian" environment. Instead, I met the very people I anticipated meeting in Vladivostok, as well as second- and third-generation Koreans, Kazaks, Indians, Dungan Chinese, and even a Mexican.

As a global church with a global vision, we serve the God of the whole world, whose power and love both transcend all cultures and redeem them. John's Revelation shows us the result of that power and love. It is here that we find the fullest vision of God's intention for creation, the fullest embodiment of what it means to be a global church.

Zooming Out

God's people are scattered all across the face of the earth. This truth is easier to grasp in theory than it is in practice. Though our world has grown smaller due to advances in technology, and globalization now seems to be the norm, our daily lives—especially the spiritual aspect of our lives—remain tied to home. Our local congregation is often the center of our spiritual universe, as well it should be. Christian faith is best formed and nurtured in the context of personal relationships. We move along the road of sanctification by walking with others who may be ahead of us on the journey, even as we turn to bring others up from behind. Ours is a journey of days spent in worship and Bible study, small groups and community service, bake sales and building funds. It is not difficult for the lens of our spiritual lives to be set on zoom, rather than wide angle.

This zoom-lens perspective can affect our understanding of the larger church as well. It is easy to take our perception of what the church looks like in our own area (the zoom-lens approach) and simply enlarge the picture. This enlarged version of our own congregation then becomes our understanding of the worldwide church. Whatever the church looks like in our own experience is extrapolated to be what the church looks like—or should look like—everywhere.

Yet, a wide-angle lens provides a very different view. From this perspective, we can see that the Wesleyan Methodist family is a global one, more than 80 million strong scattered across 130 different countries. Much like a rain forest whose trees have inter-twining roots, so it is with the Methodist Wesleyan family. Our roots grow deep into the soil not only of the movement launched by John Wesley, but of the church universal across the centuries. And our branches grow upward and outward in a great and varied canopy that stretches across the planet on which God has scattered us. The United Methodist branch of this Wesleyan Methodist family tree—12.3 million of us scattered across fifty-three different coun-tries (7.2 million in North America)—grows from those same roots and is a vital part of that same canopy. But none of this is visible with a zoom lens, it can only be seen with a wide angle.

The wide-angle perspective also enables us to see God's larger mission in the world: to bring all-encompassing healing and restora-tion to all of creation, both now and into eternity. This is the mission into which the church is called to join. As Christians, we serve "one God, the Father, by whom all things were created, and for whom we live. And . . . one Lord, Jesus Christ, through whom all things were created, and through whom we live" (1 Cor. 8:6 NLT). This creating, redeeming, and sustaining God is not limited by geography, culture, or time, but is in indeed God of the diaspora—the scattered tribe. The church is to be a co-laborer through the power of the Holy Spirit, becoming a channel through which God's healing salvation can be experienced and God's mission for all creation fulfilled.

Scattered

At one time all the people of the world spoke the same language and used the same words. As the people migrated to the east, they found a plain in the land of Babylonia and settled there. They began saying to each other, "Let's make bricks and harden them with fire." . . . Then they said, "Come, let's build a great city for ourselves with a tower that reaches into the sky. This will make us famous *and keep us from being scattered all over the world*" (Gen. 11:1–4 NLT, emphasis mine).

You likely remember the rest of the story. Their arrogance angers God and he puts a halt to their monument-building by confusing their language and scattering them across the face of the earth. The temptation of Babel is to resist God's scattering, assuming that one's own culture and language is the fullest expression of God's intent for all creation. That is what happened in the story: the people of Babel raised their own culture and language as an idol and began building a monument to it.

Yet God's mission of world redemption looks quite different. It is a pattern of scattering and blessing. We can see it clearly when God undertakes this mission through Abraham. He must leave to release God's blessing on all the nations. If Abraham leaves his native land and family, then God will bless him and all the families of the earth through him (see Genesis 12:1–3). Jesus culminates this sending out. He is the Messiah, the son of Abraham who gives his followers a mandate that encompasses all the nations: Go! Scatter to the ends of the earth. Be a blessing and all the nations of the earth will be blessed through you (see Matthew 1:1–16; 28:18–20).

Divine blessing is imprinted on the scattering of God's people. As we pass on God's blessing, we become channels through which God's redemptive action flows. Further, when we scatter, we open ourselves to the possibility that God may be using other languages and cultures as a means of blessing and redeeming our own. When, as the global body of Christ, we recognize that we are the diaspora, not the center, the Holy Spirit is given freedom to work in *all* directions and the gifts of each are made available to all.

The Holy Spirit is moving and the church is growing all over the world. Let me give you two brief examples and a more detailed one.

First, not long ago I had the privilege of speaking to a gathering of women in Northeast Nigeria—fifteen thousand of them, not counting the men and children. This United Methodist gathering took place in an area with a predominately Islamic regional government. I had to have an interview with a governmental official who was not very pleased that I was visiting his jurisdiction.

Yet in the midst of that cultural milieu, fifteen thousand women left their homes—many of them walking for days—to be present for a week of Holy Spirit-inspired worship, dancing, and learning. Many of them came to Christ for the first time.

Second, my friend Christhard Elle pastors in the northern part of Germany. He recently sent me a picture of his latest outdoor worship service. In a culture where churches are viewed more as museums than houses of prayer and worship, the Holy Spirit has moved Christhard to follow the example of Wesley and preach in the fields and village squares.

The gospel message of salvation in Jesus Christ, the opportunity for healing and the forgiveness of sins, the sharing of Holy Communion, and the call to holiness of heart and life are being publically and visibly made known in a seemingly resistant culture. Hearts are opening, and the seeds of good news are falling on ground that is surprisingly ripe for the fullness of the gospel message.

No Need for Translation

Third, recently I joined the bishop of the Eurasia Episcopal Area of the United Methodist Church at an evangelism seminar in Kyrgyzstan, a Central Asian country along the Silk Road, the ancient trade route between China and the Mediterranean. Methodists are targeted and oppressed in this 85-percent Muslim country, yet we worshipped with great spiritual power and life, joining our voices to pray in Kyrgyz, Kazak, Russian, English, Korean, and Tamil.

During our time together, it became apparent that as we sought to share the good news of Jesus Christ in our differing contexts, we each needed something that another had. No experience or understanding of the love of God in Jesus Christ was complete in isolation. The Kyrgyz offered insights about the value of community and the importance of taking time to build relationships. The second- and third-generation Koreans offered insights about suffering and hope. With each new offering, the Holy Spirit moved to bind us more tightly together as sisters and brothers in Christ, heightening our awareness that God reigns over the whole world, not just our provincial corner of it.

In the early days of the seminar, the bishop announced that one of the participants was going to be baptized. This twenty-four-year-old young man had spent much of his life in Kyrgyzstan, but was from the Dungan people of China. As we talked, he shared that he had grown up Muslim, but felt God had his hand on him even before he was born. Upon discovering his mother was pregnant, his father pressured her to have an abortion, but she refused. Because of this defiance, my young friend's father left his mother to fend for herself and her unborn child.

Remarkably, this young man's mother raised him singlehandedly, yet throughout his life his father would come and go, offering little other than violent abuse. Despite this, my friend shared his certainty that the hand of God was on his life even though he did not understand how or why—until a Methodist pastor began discipling him at the community center where he was learning English. It was then that it became clear, and it was then that he accepted Christ for himself.

As we gathered at the swimming pool for this young man's baptism, the liturgy began in Russian. Someone began translating for the few of us from the United States, but I soon found myself moving away from the sound of the English. I did not need translation to understand what was happening, to understand that my new friend was renouncing the spiritual forces of wickedness, rejecting the powers of this world, and repenting of sin. I did not need translation to understand he was confessing Jesus Christ as his Savior, putting his whole trust in his grace, and promising to serve him as Lord. I did not need translation to silently join the bishop in praying that God would pour out the Holy Spirit on the water and on my young friend.

This young man's decision to accept Christ as his Savior and Lord came long before the seminar, in the context of the local congregation in which he was discipled. But his decision to wait to be baptized until we were gathered from so many parts of the world was, for me, a tangible sign of the larger nature of the church. We were the body of Christ, scattered across the planet, but joined in the shared sacrament of baptism for the redemption of my new friend. We were the United Methodist Church, scattered across the planet, yet connected to the holy Catholic church, apostolic and universal, whose faith has been proclaimed and lived out for two thousand years.

With each encounter with God's global church, scattered across the face of the earth, I'm led to ask again and again: What spiritual treasures are missed when we remain in our Babels? What blessings do we squander or deny to others through our centralizing pride? What insights about evangelism, discipleship, faithfulness, courage, prayer, holiness, trust, or joy do we block ourselves from receiving or giving when we live as though there was only one language and culture in all the world, or even worse, when we live as though our language and culture is the fullest expression of God's intent for all creation?

The Arc of Scattered-ness

As the global church, the integrity of our witness to the world is lodged in our willingness to leave our Babels and be scattered as part of God's redemptive plan to bless all the families of the earth.

That scattering follows an arc that began at creation, and bends through the calling of Abraham, the resurrection, Pentecost, and on to new creation.

To deepen our understanding of the way it fits into God's redemptive plan, we must follow the arc to the resurrection. One of the beliefs held by people in the Methodist Wesleyan family of Christians that binds us to the church universal, is belief in the bodily resurrection of Jesus. He may have been radically transformed, but he was still recognizable by his physical body. Encountering his physical body was the only way, in fact, that at least one of the disciples, Thomas, could believe. It was Jesus' recognizable physicality that convinced him.

That Jesus was recognizable by his physical body foreshadows a miraculous truth: on the day of resurrection, it is not only our spirits that will rise, but our bodies also—in all their varied colors, shapes, and sizes. Just as the resurrected Christ was recognizable by his physical body, even though it was undeniably transfigured, so we will be recognizable by our physical bodies, even though they will be remarkably made new—healed, transformed, restored to God's intended wholeness. This, in turn, reminds us that we don't look forward to a day when the things that make us different from others *disappear*; we look forward to an eternity in which those differences *no longer divide.*

The arc of scattered-ness continues through Pentecost, which gives us a hint as to what this eternity looks like and extends our understanding of the connection of scattered-ness to God's redemptive plan. God's good creation is filled with a vibrant abundance of peoples, cultures, and languages, many of whom were gathered in Jerusalem at Pentecost. Suddenly, through the power of God's Holy Spirit, everyone was able to hear the message of redemption. The miracle was not that all these disparate people from different cultures could hear the message in the *same* language, but that they all were able to hear the message in their *own* language. Rather than obliterate the multiplicity of languages, God preserved the goodness of each while transcending them all so that everyone understood.

We know from Pentecost that God values all our languages and delights in the plethora of cultures and ethnicities that cover the face of the earth. The United Methodist Church may be only a small fraction of the worldwide Wesleyan Methodist family, but we are a microcosm of that larger family. Did you know that French is the primary language for one out of every five United Methodists? As a matter of fact, fully 25 percent of all United Methodists have a heart language that's *not* English.

When we gather, we become a visible witness to the truth that our God delights in our uniqueness, delights in our cultures, delights in our ethnicities and languages. Greater still, when we gather, we become more than the sum of our parts because we begin to embody John's Revelation image, an image that delights in all those cultures, ethnicities, and languages, but transcends them at the same time.

A Foretaste

When we gather, we become a foretaste of God's healing salvation, a future when we will be reconciled with God and with each other. There will be no more weeping, sorrow, or death, and God will wipe the tears from every eye and make all things new.

The mission of God is to bring all-encompassing healing to the whole of creation. It is this mission which God is accomplishing through Jesus Christ in the power of the Holy Spirit, and it is this mission to which we are called to join as the global church. This involves scattering so that we might become a light to the nations, a people with a particular way of being in the world, a way that bridges culture—*transcends* culture; a way that refuses to submit to the lordship of the here and now; a way that recognizes a different set of values and goals, sees a different purpose and end to the world than what the world points to. We are to be a light to the nations, but as Christopher Wright said, "There can be no light to the nations that is not shining already in transformed lives of a holy people."[1]

As the people of God, we live in the light cast by the resurrection. Our hope is not in protective towers; it is in God the Father, who sent the Son in the power of the Holy Spirit, to bring salvation in all its dimensions, *the reconciliation of all things*, the fullness of the kingdom. The questions for each of us are: Are we willing to leave our towers of Babel to join God in that mission? Are we willing to shoulder our responsibility as a global church to scatter? And, in scattering, become a channel through which God might bless all nations, tribes, peoples, and languages? Are we willing to become a foretaste of God's all-encompassing healing and salvation?

Returning to Revelation

The faithful, too great in number to count, from every nation and tribe and people and language, are gathered around the throne and before the Lamb (see Revelation 7:9). Notably, we see in Revelation 21 that rather than God taking us out of the world to a faraway heaven, the kingdom unfolds right here as God's Holy City descends to earth. We shouldn't be surprised by this. When God instructed Abraham to leave his native land, it wasn't to go into a heavenly paradise. Instead, God called him to go into the land of Sodom. Whatever else we might say about the redemptive mission God is calling the church to join, it is not a mission of escapism. God's redemptive activity is situated in the entirety of creation; the physical universe is the context of God's new creation.

In Revelation 21 we see again that faithful people have gathered from every corner of globe: all those who are sanctified in

---

1. Christopher Wright, *The Mission of God: Unlocking the Bible's Grand Narrative* (Downers Grove, IL: InterVarsity Press, 2006), 358.

Christ Jesus, together with all those who in every place call on the name of our Lord Jesus Christ (see 1 Corinthians 1:2). God's Holy City descends to earth and a shout rings out: "Look, God's home is now among his people! He will live with them, and they will be his people. God himself will be with them. He will wipe every tear from their eyes, and there will be no more death or sorrow or crying or pain. All these things are gone forever" (Rev. 21:3–4 NLT).

God's home is now made among the people and as God transforms creation, making all things new, we discover the foundational reason for everything: the healing of the nations. Our creator God has had a purpose from the beginning and it is nothing less than the blessing of all the nations—the healing of every people group, the healing of every culture, the healing of every language.

The heart of our witness as a global church is to be a foretaste of that Revelation image. We are to be *now* what God envisions for the future: a community transformed by the power of the Holy Spirit, in which differences of culture or ethnicity or language may remain, but no longer divide nor define. We were meant to be part of a community in which healing can be experienced and lives made whole as the Holy Spirit moves to transcend and redeem each of our cultures.

Questions for Discussion and Reflection

1. The United Methodist Church is a global connection. What does that mean? How does that shape who we are as a denomination?

2. Think for a moment about the contributions that Christians of other cultures have made to the world. Can you name any?

3. What insights about the kingdom of God can only be discovered as we view it in light of other ethnicities or nationalities?

4. Have you ever visited a church service in which you were the minority or could not understand the language? What was it like?

5. What would you list as the values that should bind all Christians together, even if they speak different languages or come from different countries? Should that differ from the things we have in common with Christians in our own communities?

6. How might pursuing opportunity to worship with people of different backgrounds be, in itself, a witness to others?

7. Read Revelation 7:9–10. What does this vision teach us about the nature of the coming kingdom?

8. In what practical ways can the future Methodism return to a culture that offers salvation to the lost and good news to the poor?

WITNESS

Agenda at the Crossroads

Jerry Kulah

Global United Methodism is at a crossroads and it has to decide a path to its future. The prophet Jeremiah declared, "This is what the LORD says: 'Stand at the crossroads and look; ask for the ancient paths, ask where the good way is, and walk in it, and you will find rest for your souls'" (Jer. 6:16).

A crossroads is a place of decision-making on your life's journey, where you make critical choices that might impact your life forever. It is a place where you either decide for God or against God; where you choose to follow God or follow your own gratification. At the crossroads of life, you are asked to do four things.

Stand: To stand means to be spiritually alert, culturally sensitive, socially adaptable, intellectually informed, and to give careful attention to what God is doing in this time and season so that we might become a productive part of it. As soldiers of the Lord's army, the apostle Paul enjoins us to "stand firm. Let nothing move you. Always give yourselves fully to the work of the Lord, because you know that your labor in the Lord is not in vain" (1 Cor. 15:58).

Look: The word *look* means "to observe, to take account of, to perceive, to discern and to understand." We must have a clear vision for a better tomorrow. As we look from a global perspective, what do we see? Do we see a growing or a declining church? Do we see leadership that is vision-driven and evangelistically minded in pursuit of the purpose of God? Do we see spiritually healthy and growing pastors and members, or people who are spiritually ill and in need of a "balm from Gilead" to heal their sin-sick souls? God is calling upon all of us to move forward with God's agenda for the nations. And that agenda is to be the good news of God's salvation to a world in need of hope and healing.

Ask: At the crossroads, God invites us to ask for the "ancient paths . . . the good way" (Jer. 6:16). This is the way that leads to rest for our souls; the way that leads to love, peace, and reconciliation with God and with one another. Just as God led the Israelites from Egypt to the Promised Land by a pillar of cloud by day and a pillar of fire by night (see Exodus 13:21-22), God is ever ready to lead us if we will ask him. When we ask, we shall receive (see Matthew 7:7). Therefore, let us ask the Lord for the ancient path that leads the church to righteousness, peace, and joy in the Holy Ghost; let us ask the Lord for the way that leads the church to genuine repentance and submission to the will of God; and let us pursue the ancient path that leads us to making disciples of Jesus Christ for the transformation of the Word.

Walk: God invites us to walk upon the ancient path. The ancient path is the holy, undiluted, and infallible Word of God (see Psalm 19:7-11; 2 Timothy 3:16-17). It is the living and active Word of God that is sharper than any double-edged sword; it is the Holy Scripture that penetrates the soul and spirit, and judges the thoughts and attitudes of the heart (see Hebrews 4:12). The Word of God provides us guidance and direction into the future. As the psalmist David points out, "Your word is a lamp for my feet, a light on my path" (Ps. 119:105). God expects us to believe and obey so that we might "be prosperous and successful" (Josh. 1:8).

While we live within diverse cultures and religious worldviews, it is important that we love and embrace everyone, but we must continually live within God's parameter of grace defined by Scripture. Furthermore, we must endeavor to develop Christ-centered, mission-minded, and Holy Spirit-empowered leadership across our church that is committed to making disciples of Jesus Christ for the transformation of the world. When we do these things, not only will we experience a new beginning, but the Holy Spirit of God will birth a season of revival amongst us.

What Comes Next?

Keith Boyette

A s members of the body of Christ, we live in a time of enormous potential for God's kingdom to break out in power. But
we also live in a time when the church, in far too many places, has
become lukewarm, even cold, devoid of the presence and activity
of God. In the midst of these perilous times, God has raised up a
group of believers who are committed to sharing with others the
truths entrusted to the faithful and to spreading the Word of God
throughout the world so that not one might perish.

The Wesleyan Covenant Association is a community of highly
committed Christ-followers who are fully devoted to Jesus and his
mission in a world that is deeply hurting. You have read their heart-
felt convictions in the preceding chapters of this book. We promote
ministry that combines a high view of Scripture, the lordship of
Christ, personal and social holiness, the reality that the world is
indeed our parish, Wesleyan vitality, orthodox theology, and Holy
Spirit-empowerment. Together, we long to witness to the transforming power of God to change and redeem lives and societies. We
desire nothing less than the maturity of the kingdom of God fully
present in our lives and communities.

We are emerging from a season when vital aspects of the United
Methodist Church seem to have become captive to institutionalism,
self-preservation, and cultural accommodation. In some places, the
mission has been sacrificed at the altar of a human agenda. In other

places, unity has been raised up as an idol to be worshipped. In still other places, holiness is devoid of meaning, sin is rationalized and encouraged, and a god is worshipped who is powerless to provide victory, transformation, and new life to those who earnestly seek the way, the truth, and the life. Indeed, many lost and struggling persons enter our churches and are not offered new life in Christ and the hope of salvation.

Irreconcilable differences exist in the United Methodist Church. As Jeff Greenway, pastor of Reynoldsburg United Methodist Church and chair of the Council of the Wesleyan Covenant Association, has observed, "We use the same words, quote the same scriptures, cite the same Wesley sermons, say we are committed to the same *Book of Discipline*, but we are speaking about entirely different expressions of Christianity and church." In such a place of confusion and conflict, the Wesleyan Covenant Association is prepared to resource the body of Christ with sound theology, orthodox and time-tested exposition and application of the Bible, and commitment to disciplines that are a means of grace through which God can accomplish his purposes. We have shared a portion of what we believe in this book. We desire to present all people with the timeless truth of the gospel in the person and work of Jesus Christ.

We are "Methodists"—a term of derision applied by observers to describe John Wesley and those who were disciplined in chasing after God. We believe in order, and we serve a God who is continually bringing order to the chaos of human existence. But at our best, we are a movement of God.

We resonate with the words of Wesley: "Give me one hundred preachers who fear nothing but sin, and desire nothing but God, and I care not a straw whether they be clergymen or laymen; such alone will shake the gates of hell and set up the kingdom of heaven on Earth."[1]

---

1. http://wesley.nnu.edu/john-wesley/the-letters-of-john-wesley/wesleys-letters-1777/.

We are fervently seeking awakening—of individuals, of churches, and of communities. It's in our DNA. God has given us a passion for all that is significant to him. We hear God's cry that we would cast our nets on the other side and we are eager to experience the nets becoming so full that we would be fearful of them breaking apart from the presence of Jesus, the Lord of the harvest.

This is a time of great uncertainty for many in the United Methodist Church. For some, fear abounds. What will the future look like? Will the conflicts that have sapped the church of its vitality continue to be waged? Will the church continue to grow older without connecting with the rising generations of believers? Will we continue to be held captive by an institution focused on perpetuating itself more than the mission of the gospel?

For others, there is an urgency which borders on rashness. How long do we remain connected to a denomination where it seems as if some leaders do not honor God's Word and doctrines are taught that are opposite to the orthodox tenets of the Christian faith that have stood the tests of time? Are we permitting our concern about property to limit our ability to be obedient? Are we better advised to seek an orderly departure from the United Methodist Church into whatever is next as we demonstrate to the world that we can disagree in love and release one another for the sake of mission? Or do our principles compel us to move ahead regardless of devastation left in the wake of such a decision?

The Wesleyan Covenant Association is actively preparing in this climate of uncertainty for what will emerge as the next Methodism. The days are growing short for God's deliverance. His people will not be in bondage, oppressed forever. We don't know the precise form of God's deliverance. Perhaps the United Methodist Church will be radically transformed and renewed so that it recaptures the focus and fruitfulness of its most effective days when it delivered the uncompromised gospel to a hurting and hungry world. Perhaps God will raise up a faithful church out of the ashes of what has gone before. Or perhaps God will do something new, which we are not able to envision at this time. Nevertheless, the Wesleyan Covenant Association is actively positioning itself before God to be ready to move as the Holy Spirit directs and empowers.

We are confident that just as God had plans for the Israelites in exile in Babylon (see Jeremiah 29:11), he has plans for us. We are confident that those are plans for good and not for disaster, to give us a future and a hope. We are resolute in prayer, knowing that God hears us. We wholeheartedly look for his direction and provision, confident that we will find him, and trust that he will lead us out of this present time and restore our fortunes. God will make his name famous in and through us.

In many places, well-meaning believers are unaware of the conflict that will impact their local church, the health of believers, and the salvation of those who are far from God. Engaging the future demands courage and great faith from each of us on this journey. Now is not the time for fear and timidity. No, God has given us a spirit of power, love, and self-discipline. We trust you will use this book and the accompanying materials to be equipped to spell out a vision for the next Methodism. Understand that the theological division within the denomination goes to the very core of what it means for us to be the bride of Christ. Unless our foundation is strong, we are vulnerable to every wind and wave that crashes in the storm. But if we listen and obey what God has revealed to us in the core teachings of the faith addressed here, though the rain comes in torrents and the floodwaters rise and the winds beat against us, we won't collapse because our faith has been built on bedrock that God has established (see Matthew 7:24–25).

What Can You Do?

- Share this book and resources with your friends.
- Pray and fast. The Bible assures us that "the earnest prayer of a righteous person has great power and produces wonderful results" (James 5:16 NLT).

- Build a team where you are planted so that you can be God's witness in your church and community. Engage others who may not be aware of what is at stake in this season. Don't get distracted. We are contending for the core doctrines of the church, which have been addressed in these pages.
- Walk the walk. Live a life that brings honor to God and makes him present in the lives of others.
- Get connected. We invite you to join with others who are contending for the faith through the Wesleyan Covenant Association by becoming a member of the WCA and associating with a regional chapter in your area. Take advantage of the many resources and gatherings made available by the WCA (www.wesleyancovenant.org).
- Persevere. Don't become weary or discouraged. The future belongs to the Lord. You have come to the kingdom for such a time as this (see Esther 4:14).
- Know that you are not alone. Persons in every conference in every jurisdictional and central conference are joined with you at this vital crossroads. Receive this blessing, written by the author of Hebrews:

> Now may the God of peace—who brought up from the dead our Lord Jesus, the great Shepherd of the sheep, and ratified an eternal covenant with his blood—may he equip you with all you need for doing his will. May he produce in you, through the power of Jesus Christ, every good thing that is pleasing to him. All glory to him forever and ever! Amen. (13:20-21 NLT)

Questions for Discussion and Reflection

1. What has struck you most deeply from the past weeks of study and discussion?
2. What does it mean to you to live out your Christian faith as a Wesleyan Methodist?

3. Do you feel comfortable in your current setting identifying where you fall on the spectrum of beliefs currently present in the United Methodist Church?

4. Do your relationships with fellow believers include respect so that viewpoints that might differ can be expressed with transparency and love?

5. What parts of living as a Methodist are most near and dear to your heart? What parts of living as a Methodist do you see as essential, and what parts as nonessential?

6. What is one hope you have for your local community of faith, and for the denomination it belongs to?

About the Writers

William J. Abraham is the Albert J. Outler Professor of Wesley Studies at Southern Methodist University's Perkins School of Theology and an ordained elder in the Southwest Texas Conference of the United Methodist Church.

Jorge Acevedo is the lead pastor of Grace Church, a multi-site, United Methodist congregation in Southwest Florida with five campuses (Cape Coral, Fort Myers Shores, Fort Myers Central, Fort Myers Trinity, and Sarasota in Southwest Florida).

Keith Boyette is the president of the Wesley Covenant Association. Boyette is a member of the Virginia Annual Conference and founded the Wilderness Community United Methodist Church before joining WCA as its first president.

Maxie Dunnam is the former president and chancellor of Asbury Theological Seminary. He is now senior pastor emeritus and executive director of CCGlobal at Christ United Methodist Church in Memphis.

Andrew Forrest is the founding pastor of Munger Place Church in Dallas, Texas, daughter church of Highland Park United Methodist Church.

Jeff Greenway is the senior pastor of Reynoldsburg United Methodist Church in Reynoldsburg, Ohio. He is the chair of the Wesleyan Covenant Association Council.

Madeline Carrasco Henners has served as a pastor in the south Texas area for eleven years and is currently appointed to First UMC La Grange, Texas.

Heather Hill is the director of community life at Mosaic United Methodist Church in Evans, Georgia.

Jerry Kulah is the dean of the Gbarnga School of Theology at the United Methodist University, Liberia.

Kenneth Levingston is the senior pastor of Jones Memorial United Methodist Church in Houston, Texas.

Carolyn Moore is the founding and lead pastor of Mosaic United Methodist Church in Evans, Georgia.

Debo Onabanjo is the pastor of Zion United Methodist Church in Toledo, Ohio.

Carlos Pirona is a graduate and current president of the Seminario Wesleyano de Venezuela, founded in 2002. He is also the founding pastor of the Restauracion Internacional UMC de Venezuela, the largest UMC in Venezuela.

Kimberly Reisman is executive director of World Methodist Evangelism and an elder in the United Methodist Church.

Chris Ritter is directing pastor of Geneseo First United Methodist Church in Illinois and the director of the Geneseo First-Cambridge Multisite Ministry.

David Watson serves as academic dean and professor of New Testament at United Theological Seminary in Dayton, Ohio.

Acknowledgments

We are indebted to the many strong voices and wise souls who worked to put this resource together. The authors of these pages invested many hours and much wisdom, and each of them did so with a generous spirit. Steve Beard, the lead editor of this project, labored faithfully to create a unified voice out of a dozen manuscripts and deserves our profoundest gratitude. This would not have been possible without his care and passion. Our deep appreciation to Andy Miller and the Seedbed Farm Team for overseeing this project, and to Elizabeth Glass-Turner, Jessica LaGrone, and the staff of Asbury Theological Seminary for collaborating on the production of the video segments. Our prayers and encouragement go to churches around the country that are dedicated to living out an orthodox Wesleyan faith that is alive and fruitful. May God bless you richly as you talk together about what it means to follow Jesus.

—Members of the Wesleyan Covenant Association Council

2017

CPSIA information can be obtained
at www.ICGtesting.com
Printed in the USA
LVOW03s0745280218
568038LV00004B/4/P